Changing Values in College

An Exploratory Study of the Impact of College Teaching

By PHILIP E. JACOB, Ph.D.

Professor of Political Science
University of Pennsylvania

H B

HARPER & BROTHERS PUBLISHERS NEW YORK

Changing Values
in College

Contents

Introduction by Paul J. Braisted   vii

Foreword   xi

Summary of Findings   1

 I. Values of American College Students   12
    The common values—Issues which divide

 II. Value-outcomes of a College Education   38
    From diversity to uniformity, acquiring the college out-
    look—Towards flexibility and sociability—The myth
    of college liberalism—The constancy of basic values—
    The college impact on religion

III. Influence of the Curriculum   58
    What you study does not determine your values—
    Does liberal education not liberalize?—The impact
    of programs of general education on beliefs, on
    critical thinking, on value goals—The specific effect
    of social science courses—Student evalutions

IV. Impact of the Instructor   78
    The low esteem of students for the instructor—Where
    faculty count—The teacher's role in programs of
    general education

 V. Effects of Teaching Methods   88
    Student-centered teaching—The significance of dis-
    cussion—Education through experience, laboratory
    practices and the problem approach

50504

VI. The Peculiar Potency of Some Colleges   99
     A Record of liberalism—Personality differences—Dis-
     tinctive value-profiles—The nature of the institu-
     tional thrust

VII. Student Personality—A Filter of Educational Values   117
     The "doing" motivation vs. general education—The
     disposition to conform—The "authoritarian person-
     ality" as a college student

     A Note on Further Inquiry   130

     Inventory of the Data   138

Introduction

THIS study has been full of surprises which may be of interest to its readers.

Originally it was visualized as an effort to find more reliable evidence concerning the outcomes of teaching general education courses in the social sciences. It was a continuation of early consultations, studies and publications. Professor Philip Jacob and his committee wisely decided to find out what other efforts had already been made as a prelude to development of a modest research project. First surprise—much more had been attempted than even the best informed realized. Assembly of this data became a major task of the director and the research study was necessarily postponed. He was led afield across the country consulting with many educators and studying numerous reports and files of unpublished materials.

The results of this exploratory endeavor are to be found in an "Inventory," pp. 138-174 comprising several hundred items varying widely in purpose, scope, and significance. The wealth of this data presents the reader, as it did the director, with major difficulties. These are due to the diversity of methods used, the variety of courses and teaching methods studied, the differences between small local studies and comprehensive, extensive, well-staffed research programs. Then, too, there is always the fundamental problem of definition, what is being studied and what methods are appropriate. The limitations of all this activity are inescapable.

Confronted with this situation the director, with no little courage but with scholarly competence and sensitivity, decided to see what meaning could be found in this activity. This involved, on the one hand, devising a framework in which to summarize the evidence, and, on the other, trying to interpret it for what it might be worth. The results are to be found in the "Inventory" and the chapters of this report.

Then came the second surprise—the findings were for the most part shockingly but inescapably negative although in part significantly positive. The director was encouraged to report this with scholarly candor.

The trustees were as puzzled as the director and his committee with these findings and so decided to ask other educators with differing experience and competences to appraise the report. Publication was postponed and a preliminary printing arranged. The report was sent to all whose studies were listed in the "Inventory" and selected members of several national educational associations, a total of about six hundred educators. A personal letter asked for a candid appraisal of the report, the findings, and the suggestions for further inquiry which formed one chapter. Additional copies were offered in limited quantity for colleagues for similar individual or group appraisal. Came the next surprise—a vigorous, prompt and widespread interest manifest in hundreds of requests for additional copies of this report, and, later on, more than one hundred and fifty thoughtful letters of comment.

Publication of the report is a direct response to the unsolicited but insistent demand of these first readers.

The biggest surprise of all was the degree to which the report stimulated discussion, not merely about the immediate concerns of the report, but about the most fundamental questions of educational purpose, objectives, and research. Why was this? Our correspondence suggests that it is explained in part by the shock effect of negative findings concerning many long-cherished but little-examined assumptions of rival programs and theories of higher education.

Most readers reported, however, that they recovered quickly from the shock, found corroboration in their reading or experience, but became troubled about the unexamined rival claims of institutions and educators. Probably it is this provocative and controversial aspect of the report which has chiefly affected the response. Who could wish for more than that fundamental questions be asked—and debated!

The range of issues under discussion may be illustrated by the following examples. Is there some fault or shortcoming in research methodology in this field? How can research procedures be refined, or new ones imaginatively devised, so as to learn more about the outcomes of our educational endeavors? Can a "value" be abstracted for critical examination, or has its essence been changed by such effort? What value or values, what outcomes in attitudes and commitments, should a college appropriately seek? What is the relative significance of intellectual, aesthetic, moral, social, or religious values as outcomes of college experience? What, after all, is the role of the teacher, not merely the outstanding person a few of whom we have each known, but the average good teacher? Why is it that certain teachers and certain institutions have a marked influence upon a wide range of values of many students? Whatever one's special concern or responsibility in higher education, surely these are the most relevant questions to ask in a time of great ferment and expansion.

Some of the studies reported are continuing and others are being developed. New evidence will undoubtedly enrich the discussions. The Hazen Foundation will continue the study hoping thereby to supplement other efforts in a modest way. The report of the exploratory study is now published for any and all who are interested in the direction of higher education. We will welcome candid comment from readers who may wish to share their reflections.

We welcome this opportunity to thank the members of the advisory committee, the University of Pennsylvania who spared Dr. Jacob for this work, and all who assisted him in countless ways. We are grateful to Philip Jacob and admire the scholarly competence, imagination, and sensitivity with which he fulfilled a difficult assignment. We have abundant evidence that the "first readers" join in thanking him for the assembled data and his stimulating interpretation.

New Haven, Connecticut
October 1957.

Paul J. Braisted, President
The Hazen Foundation

Foreword

THIS study was undertaken to discover what happens to the values held by American college students as a result of the general education they secure in social science.

It is an outgrowth of a survey, conducted in 1951-1952 by Professor John Moore of Swarthmore College, of the place of religious and moral values in programs of general education at twenty-six institutions. Professor Moore found the social sciences "characterized by great ambiguity and confusion with regard to value problems." He urged more detailed study of the aims, rationale, and effects on student beliefs and conduct, of the instruction provided in the introductory courses and other parts of the curriculum fulfilling an integrative, or general, educational function. His report, *The Place of Moral and Religious Values in Programs of General Education*, was printed by the Edward W. Hazen Foundation, under whose auspices both his survey and the present one have been conducted.

Most colleges and universities today feel responsible for the "liberal" education of all their students, even those who have already set sights on professional or technical careers. What this means in curricular terms varies from requiring a student to select a distribution of standard basic courses in natural sciences, the humanities and the social sciences, to having him take a planned sequence of work which aims to comprehend and integrate the major fields of knowledge.

A common assumption lies back of these commitments to a general education higher than that furnished by high schools, an assumption that there are civilizing values which need to be communicated to and through any person who goes to college and expects to live primarily by means of a trained mind. There are important differences in emphasis and even substance in the value-goals espoused by educators. But few deny that they expect college to exert a "maturing" influence upon students' standards of behavior, quality of judgment, sense of social responsibility, and perspicacity of understanding of themselves and others, in addition to whatever body of skills and facts they acquire.

This purposefulness with regard to value-outcomes has been apparent in many of the post-war reappraisals and self-studies of American institutions of higher learning. Curricula have been redesigned, new programs and courses of study conceived, or the proportion of required humanistic studies increased with a view to making more potent the liberalizing impact of undergraduate education. Most faculty and administrative officers would probably concede that there are strict limits beyond which teaching cannot and should not go in the inculcation of values, and that, in the main, students' values are more influenced by family, friends and fraternities than by the courses they take. Nevertheless, the argument runs strong that values are *both* caught *and* taught. In this view, the teacher cannot dodge responsibility for the communication of values—civic, intellectual, ethical and, in church-related colleges, religious. He should therefore become more self-conscious about his value role, clarify his goals, and evaluate realistically the outcomes of his teaching in terms of changes of belief and behavior on the part of his students.

The import of this orientation to values as educational goals has borne with particular force upon the humanities and the social sciences, whose subject matter is human behavior and which therefore inescapably confront value issues. How should such issues be introduced to students? How deeply should students be invited to probe, to challenge, and to espouse in areas of controversy? Just what is the teacher's obligation to encourage good citizenship, critical thinking, or moral character? Such questions especially preoccupy those charged with conducting the main introductory courses, as they try to determine a syllabus and handle a section of freshmen and sophomores in a way which will contribute to a worthy "general education."

THE FOCUS OF THIS STUDY

The central problem of this study has been to see what changes do occur in students' patterns of value during college, and to what extent such changes stem from exposure to various types of social science instruction in the "general" part of the curriculum.

The study presumes that values inhere in and are inseparable from the teaching of social science. They are a *subject* of instruction. They are sometimes a specific *motivation* of instruction. They are also a *consequence* of instruction—though to what extent and in what way is broadly the concern of this research.

Despite the methodological difficulties of social science research in the field of values, the group planning this study was convinced that an empirical approach to the problem should be followed. They conceived of "values" or "value-patterns" as *preferences, criteria or choices of personal or group conduct.* A value in this sense is a standard for decision-making, held by an individual student, and normally to be identified when it is articulated in (a) an expressed verbal statement or (b) overt conduct.

Such an approach to the study of values implies examination both of the actual behavioral choices of students and of the structure of beliefs to which such choices are related. The impact of social science curricula upon a student's conviction of what man is, and the nature of the world in which men live, might be a vital factor in altering his choices of conduct. Hence, it was equally the concern of this study to identify an *action-result* representing a change in values, and to discover any *fundamental alteration of beliefs* which might lie behind it, or anticipate it.

The inquiry has concentrated upon curricular, as distinct from "extra-curricular" or "co-curricular" influences upon students' value-patterns. It has been primarily concerned with that part of the curriculum which fulfills a general education function in the social sciences, namely courses which take seriously the problem of educating the student who does not intend to specialize in a social science subject. These include (a) courses providing a general introduction to the whole field of social science, offered inter-departmentally or without specific departmental responsibility, (b) basic departmental courses which are generally required of all students, or fulfill a social science divisional requirement—in economics, sociology, history, political science, anthropology, or psychology, (c) senior or other "integrating" courses.

As the study progressed, the network of interlocking factors affecting students' values became increasingly apparent, so the focus was extended to include elements beyond the actual content and organization of courses—such as the impact of the instructor, of various methods of teaching, and of the character or "climate" of particular institutions. Furthermore, consideration had to be given to student personality characteristics which might account for the markedly different responses of students to similar types of educational influence.

Specifically, we have surveyed data relevant to the following questions:

(1) What are the main contemporary patterns of value among American students?

What values are held in common by most students?

On what values do they seem to differ?

Are there characteristic differences in the values held by students at different types of institutions or at colleges in different parts of the country?

(2) How much of an overall difference does the college experience make in students' values?

How much do students' values change during college?

Which values are most malleable and which relatively stable?

How fundamental are these changes and how persistent?

How general are the changes?

Are the changes significantly different or greater than in American society at large?

(3) How much are students' values influenced by the content of the instruction they receive, particularly in social science?

How much of a difference does a liberal, instead of a vocational or pre-professional, curriculum make?

How potent is the effect of social science courses, especially those which fulfill a general education function?

Do some types of courses have a more significant effect than others?

Does the content or organization of courses affect their outcome?

(4) What impact is attributable to the instructor?

Can one distinguish between faculty on the basis of their influence upon students' values?

(5) Do changes in students' values reflect the methods by which they have been taught?

Are certain techniques more potent than others in influencing values?

(6) Does a more significant development of values occur at some institutions than at others? If so, what characterizes these potent institutions?

(7) To what extent does a student's type of personality filter his college education and control its effect upon his values?

Do certain types of students respond more significantly to some forms or methods of general education than do others?

DEVELOPMENT OF THE STUDY

The plan of the study envisaged an exploratory stage, and a possible experimental stage.

The present report culminates the exploratory stage. It is based upon a selective survey of programs of instruction which were thought to be of special significance from the standpoint of affecting students' values. This included on-the-spot observation of the programs at some thirty institutions, and the gathering of a substantial body of evaluative data on courses and curricula at these and other colleges and universities. The institutions varied greatly in size, location, administration and objectives. The generous cooperation as unofficial consultants of more than a hundred leading educators and specialists in evaluation has been indispensable in the conduct of the survey.

The study is especially indebted to the directors of the American Council on Education's Cooperative Study of Evaluation in General Education and to the Cornell University Social Science Research Center for making available important data from their respective inventories of student attitudes and values.

The following group generously undertook to work closely with the Director in planning and guiding the study. Their wide practical experience with college teaching, sensitive understanding of students, familiarity with the methods and problems of this kind of research, and shrewd insights concerning the whole question of values in human relationships were brought to bear upon the project at each key stage of its development. But the Director must be held responsible for the final formulation of the findings and the contents of the report.

Irwin Abrams, Professor of History, Antioch College
Paul J. Braisted, President, The Hazen Foundation

A. J. Brumbaugh, Director, Council for the Study of Higher Education in Florida

W. Rex Crawford, Professor of Sociology, University of Pennsylvania

Roderic H. Davison, Professor of European History, George Washington University

Loyd D. Easton, Professor of Philosophy, Ohio Wesleyan University

John A. Hutchison, Professor of Religion, Columbia University

Robert H. Knapp, Associate Professor of Psychology, Wesleyan University

Donald Meiklejohn, Associate Professor of Philosophy, University of Chicago

John M. Moore, Professor of Philosophy and Religion, Swarthmore College

Ira De A. Reid, Professor of Sociology, Haverford College

Changing Values
in College

Summary of Findings

In CAPSULE form these are the tentative conclusions reached in the study:

A PROFILE OF THE VALUES OF AMERICAN COLLEGE STUDENTS

The values of American college students are remarkably homogeneous, considering the variety of their social, economic, ethnic, racial, and religious backgrounds, and the relatively unrestricted opportunities they have had for freedom of thought and personal development.

A dominant characteristic of students in the current generation is that they are *gloriously contented* both in regard to their present day-to-day activity and their outlook for the future. Few of them are worried—about their health, their prospective careers, their family relations, the state of national or international society or the likelihood of their enjoying secure and happy lives. They are supremely confident that their destinies lie within their own control rather than in the grip of external circumstances.

The great majority of students appear unabashedly *self-centered*. They aspire for material gratifications for themselves and their families. They intend to look out for themselves first and expect others to do likewise.

But this is not the individualistic self-centeredness of the pioneer. American students fully accept the conventions of the contemporary business society as the context within which they will realize their personal desires. They cheerfully expect to conform to the economic status quo and to receive ample rewards for dutiful and productive effort. They anticipate no die-hard struggle for survival of the fittest as each seeks to gratify his own desires, but rather an abundance for all as each one teams up with his fellow self-seekers in appointed places on the American assembly-line.

Social harmony with an *easy tolerance of diversity* pervades the student environment. Conformists themselves, the American students see little need to insist that each and every person be and behave just like themselves. They are for the most part (with some allowance for sectional difference) ready to live in a mobile society, without racial, ethnic or income barriers. But they do not intend to crusade for non-discrimination, merely to accept it as it comes, a necessary convention in a homogenized culture.

The traditional *moral virtues are valued* by almost all students. They respect sincerity, honesty, loyalty, as proper standards of conduct for decent people. But they are not inclined to censor those who choose to depart from these canons. Indeed they consider laxity a prevalent phenomenon, even more prevalent than the facts seem to warrant. Nor do they feel personally bound to unbending consistency in observing the code, especially when a lapse is socially sanctioned. For instance, standards are generally low in regard to academic honesty, systematic cheating being a common practice rather than the exception at many major institutions.

Students normally express a *need for religion* as a part of their lives and make time on most weekends for an hour in church. But there is a "ghostly quality" about the beliefs and practices of many of them, to quote a sensitive observer. Their religion does not carry over to guide and govern important decisions in the secular world. Students expect these to be socially determined. God has little to do with the behavior of men in society, if widespread student judgment be accepted. His place is in church and perhaps in the home, not in business or club or community. He is worshipped, dutifully and with propriety, but the campus is not permeated by a live sense of His presence.

American students are likewise *dutifully responsive towards government*. They expect to obey its laws, pay its taxes, serve in its armed forces—without complaint but without enthusiasm. They will discharge the obligations demanded of them though they will not voluntarily contribute to the public welfare. Nor do they particularly desire an influential voice in public policy. Except for the ritual of voting, they are content to abdicate the citizen's role in the political process and to leave to others the effective power of governmental decision. They are politically irresponsible, and often politically illiterate as well.

This disposition is reflected in *strangely contradictory attitudes towards international affairs*. Students predict another major war within a dozen years yet international problems are the least of the concerns to which they expect to give much personal attention during their immediate future. The optimism with which they view their prospects for a good long life belies the seriousness of their gloomy prophecy. They readily propose some form of supra-national government as a means of preventing war, but a very large number display only a limited knowledge of and confidence in the United Nations as an instrument of cooperative international action.

Turning to their immediate preoccupation, the pursuit of an education, students by and large *set great stock by college* in general and their own college in particular. The intensity of their devotion varies quite a bit with the institution and sometimes with the nature of the students' educational goals. And the real point of the devotion is not the same for all. Only a minority seem to value their college education primarily in terms of its intellectual contribution, or its nurturing of personal character and the capacity for responsible human relationships. Vocational preparation, and skill and experience in social "adjustment" head the rewards which students crave from their higher education.

These values are not the unanimous choice of American college students. The available data indicate that the profile just given may apply to 75 per cent or 80 per cent of them. In the remaining minority are individuals who forcefully refute some or all of the generalizations. Furthermore, on some issues students have no common mind—for instance, on how much discipline children should have, how much government the country needs, how far power should be relied on in international affairs and to what extent political dissidence should be repressed for the sake of national security. But for the most part, a campus "norm" of values prevails in the 1950's, coast to coast, at state university or denominational college, for the Ivy Leaguer or the city college commuter.

Against the background of earlier generations, these values of today's students look different. The undergirding of the Puritan heritage on which the major value assumptions of American society have rested is inconspicuous, if it is present at all. Perhaps these students are the forerunners of a major cultural and ethical revolution, the unconscious ushers of an essentially secular (though nominally religious), self-oriented (though group-conforming) society.

VALUE-OUTCOMES OF A COLLEGE EDUCATION

The main overall effect of higher education upon student values is to bring about general acceptance of a body of standards and attitudes characteristic of college-bred men and women in the American community.

There is more homogeneity and greater consistency of values among students at the end of their four years than when they begin. Fewer seniors espouse beliefs which deviate from the going standards than do freshmen. The student has ironed out serious conflicts of values or at least achieved a workable compromise. Throughout, no sharp break seems to occur in the continuity of the main patterns of value which the students bring with them to college. Changes are rarely drastic or sudden, and they tend to emerge on the periphery of the student's character, affecting his application of values, rather than the core of values themselves.

To call this process a *liberalization* of student values is a misnomer. The impact of the college experience is rather to *socialize* the individual, to refine, polish, or "shape up" his values so that he can fit comfortably into the ranks of American college alumni.

The values of the college graduate do differ in some respects from the rest of the society. He is more concerned with status, achievement and prestige. Proportionately more college graduates distrust "welfare economics" and "strong" government than in the country at large. Paradoxically they tend to be somewhat more tolerant and less repressive of "radical" ideas and unconventional people, also less prejudiced towards minority groups and alien cultures. They share few of the cold-war suspicions of the subversiveness of college faculties, nor do they support the popular stereotype of the colleges' godlessness. Religiously, they may be less superstitious or other-worldly than their fellow countrymen. The college man or woman thus tends to be more self-important—more conservative—more tolerant—and less fearful of evil forces in this world and outside than those who have not been "higher-educated."

It seems reasonable to credit these differences in value to the college experience, partly to its positive influence in bringing students' outlook into line with a college "standard," partly to an even more subtle selective process which ferrets out those students who are not sufficiently adaptive to acquire the distinctive value-patterns of the college graduate. Many whose values are too rigidly set in a mold at odds with the prevailing college standard apparently never consider going to college in the first place. Many of those who do enter (perhaps 50 per cent) drop out, the greater proportion probably because they have not found their experience or associations really congenial. The great majority who are left find little difficulty in making the rather modest jump which is required from the values they held in high school to college sophistication. The transition is especially easy for those with parents who went to college and are engaged in professional occupations.

The Influence of the Curriculum

This study has not discerned significant changes in student values which can be attributed directly either to the character of the curriculum or to the basic courses in social science which students take as part of their general education.

For the most part, the values and outlook of students do not vary greatly whether they have pursued a conventional liberal arts program, an integrated general education curriculum or one of the strictly professional-vocational options. The more liberally educated student may take a somewhat more active interest in community responsibilities, and keep better informed about public affairs. But the distinction is not striking and by no means does it occur consistently among students at all colleges. It does *not* justify the conclusion that a student acquires a greater maturity of judgment on issues of social policy or a more sensitive regard for the humane values because he had a larger dose of liberal or general education.

Even fundamental revisions of the formal content of the curriculum designed to confront students more forcefully with problems of personal and social conduct and to involve them in a searching examination of value-issues rarely appear to have brought about a marked difference in students' beliefs and judgments, let alone their actual patterns of conduct. Nor is there solid evidence of a delayed reaction or "sleeper effect." The alumnus of several years exhibits no unusual trademarks identifying the character of his undergraduate curriculum.

The same negative conclusion applies to the general effect of social science courses. The values expressed by those who are most interested in social sciences are little different from those of other students. This is true not only of personal moral and religious values, but also of attitudes towards social and political issues regarding which the social science students are presumably more concerned and better informed. Neither the students' interest nor their instruction in social science seems to exert a broad influence on their beliefs, or their judgments of conduct and policy.

This finding from a synoptic perspective is reinforced by the results of most attempts to measure objectively the impact of particular courses. Few social science courses have demonstrated a capacity to alter attitudes or beliefs to a much greater degree or in a different direction than in the student body as a whole at the same institution (or among "control" groups of students who were not enrolled in the particular course).

What does happen frequently as a consequence or at least a corollary of a basic introduction to one or more of the social sciences is a redirection of the academic and vocational interests of some students. They are captivated by the subject and decide to change their majors and perhaps later their careers. It is clear too that students interested in social science tend to have more appreciation for general education than for vocational preparation as an educational goal. Large numbers of students also testify that their social science courses have increased their understanding of world affairs, and interest in politics. How much weight should be given to such subjective and indefinite evaluation is questionable, however, especially when there is little evidence that actual participation in public life has been increased. A distinction in *interest*, but not in *value*, may come from basic education in the social sciences, but, contrary to some expectations, mere interest in social science does not appear to generate corresponding value judgments.

IMPACT OF THE INSTRUCTOR

Equally disturbing is evidence that the quality of teaching has relatively little effect upon the value-outcomes of general education—in the social sciences or in other fields—so far as the great mass of students is concerned.

The personality, skill and devotion of teachers to their students and their subject varies tremendously within and among institutions. So do their personal and educational philosophies, the intensity of their value-commitments, and the degree to which they deliberately pursue value-goals in class and outside.

Students, for their part, have demonstrated a capacity for shrewdly evaluating the performance of instructors. They particularly value the teacher who couples high respect for students as persons, with a capacity to arouse interest in his subject.

Yet by and large the impact of the good teacher is indistinguishable from that of the poor one, at least in terms of his influence upon the values held and cherished by his students. Students like the good teacher better, and enjoy his classes more. But their fundamental response is little different than to any one else teaching the course. With important individual exceptions, instructors seem equally *in*effective in tingling the nerve centers of students' values.

In the process of mass education, many students appear to take the instructor for granted, as he comes, good or bad, a necessary appliance in Operation College. His personal influence washes out in such an atmosphere, especially in regard to the deeper issues of life-direction, and the recognition and resolution of basic value-conflicts. A teacher can be recognized as a *good* teacher by his students, but with increasing rarity is he an *effective* teacher in the communication and maturing of values. Something in the contemporary social or educational climate curtains him off from the inner recesses of his students' character and freezes their motivational responses.

Student testimony and perceptive observation by educators and counsellors indicates, however, that *some* teachers do exert a profound influence on *some* students, even to the point of causing particular individuals to re-orient their philosophy of life and adopt new and usually more socially responsible vocational goals. What it is that ignites such influence can hardly be defined, so personal, varied, and unconscious are the factors at work. It is perhaps significant, however, that faculty identified as having this power with students are likely to be persons whose own value-commitments are firm and openly expressed, and who are out-going and warm in their personal relations with students. Furthermore, faculty influence appears more pronounced at institutions where association between faculty and students is normal and frequent, and students find teachers receptive to unhurried and relaxed conversations out of class.

EFFECTS OF TEACHING METHODS

The method of instruction seems to have only a minor influence on students' value judgments.

"Student-centered" techniques of teaching and a stress on discussion in contrast to lecture or recitation have been strongly advocated as effective means of engaging the student's personal participation in the learning process, and encouraging him to reach valid judgments of his own on important issues. Studies of the comparative effectiveness of such methods do *not* generally support such a conviction.

Under certain circumstances, notably a favorable institutional environment, student-centered teaching has apparently resulted in a somewhat more satisfactory emotional and social adjustment by the students, and a more congenial learning situation. But there is little indication of a significantly greater alteration in the beliefs or behavioral standards of students taught by one method or another.

The response of a student to a given type of instruction often reflects his personality or disposition *previous* to entering upon the course. Some students react very negatively to a more permissive teaching technique. They feel frustrated and uneasy without more direction and authority exercised by the teacher. Consequently, they may actually learn less, and be less profoundly affected by a course taught in this manner, than by a more formal, definitely structured approach. In any case, the evidence is not conclusive that the potency of general education in influencing student values may be consistently strengthened by using a particular method of teaching.

However, students are often deeply affected by participation in experiences which vividly confront them with value issues, and possibly demand decisions on their part whose consequences they can witness. As a rule, the more directly that general education in social science hooks into students' own immediate problems and links the broader value questions with which it is concerned to personal student experiences, the more significant is its impact.

THE PECULIAR POTENCY OF SOME COLLEGES

Similar as the patterns of student values appear on a mass view, the intellectual, cultural or moral "climate" of some institutions stands out from the crowd. The response of students to education within the atmosphere of these institutions is strikingly different from the national pattern.

The very individuality of these places makes comparisons unreal, but they do seem to have in common a high level of expectancy of their students. *What* is expected is *not* the same. It may be outstanding intellectual initiative and drive, profound respect for the dignity and worth of work, world-mindedness or just open-mindedness, a sense of community responsibility or of social justice, a dedication to humanitarian service, or religious faithfulness. Everyone, however, is conscious of the mission to which the institution stands dedicated, though this is not necessarily loudly trumpeted at every convocation, nor elaborated in fulsome paragraphs of aims and purposes in the college bulletin.

Where there is such unity and vigor of expectation, students seem drawn to live up to the college standard, even if it means quite a wrench from their previous ways of thought, or a break with the prevailing values of students elsewhere. The college serves as a cocoon in which a new value-orientation can mature and solidify until it is strong enough to survive as a maverick in the conventional world.

A climate favorable to a redirection of values appears more frequently at private colleges of modest enrollment. In a few instances, something of the sort has also emerged within a particular school or division of a larger public institution.

With a distinctive quality of this kind, an institution acquires a "personality" in the eyes of its students, alumni and staff. The deep loyalty which it earns reflects something more than pride, sentiment or prestige. A community of values has been created. Not that every student sees the whole world alike, but most have come to a similar concern for the values held important in their college. The hold of these institutional values evidently persists long after graduation and often influences the choice of college by the next generation.

STUDENT PERSONALITY AND EDUCATIONAL INFLUENCE

Recent research has identified certain personality characteristics of students which "filter" their educational experience.

Some students have a set of mind so rigid, an outlook on human relations so stereotyped and a reliance on authority so compulsive that they are intellectually and emotionally incapable of understanding new ideas, and seeing, much less accepting, educational implications which run counter to their pre-conceptions. This particularly limits their responsiveness in the social sciences and the humanities whenever controversial issues arise. Such students quail in the presence of conflict and uncertainty. They crave "right answers." They distrust speculative thought, their own or their fellow students'. They recoil from "creative discussion."

Under most conditions of general education, where content and teaching method have been more or less standardized to suit what faculties consider the needs of the "average" student, the personalities just described become deadwood. As an out-of-step minority, they appear impervious to a real educational experience, even though the brainier ones may survive academically by parrotting texts and instructors on examinations. Many educators have concluded that such students do not belong in college; others insist that at least some liberalizing influence may rub off on them if they are obliged to run a lengthy gauntlet of general courses in social science and humanities, distasteful as the student may find them. A few institutions, however, are exploring special approaches to general education for this type of student, with promising results.

On the basis of the limited experimentation to date, such a "remedial" approach to social education for the "stereotype-personality" appears to require: (1) a careful and impersonal technique of identifying the students in need of special attention, (2) considerable homogeneity of personality in the classroom, (3) a well-ordered syllabus with rather definite assignments and clearly stated, frequently repeated, guiding principles (at least in the earlier part of the course), (4) an instructor who has great patience, and great belief in the potentialities of *these* students, and who can sensibly combine a fair amount of personal direction with persistent and imaginative efforts to engage the students' own intellectual powers in the learning process. The instructor needs to lead these students—but not dictate to them. He needs to wean them gradually from their excessive dependence on authority, slowly increase their sense of security in the face of the new, the unexplored and the different, and nurture self-confidence and respect for their own capacities to judge and to reason independently.

Not enough is yet known to insure the general success of such teaching, and few of these students will achieve the autonomy of those whose personality was freer to start with. But they have shown striking gains in critical thinking and developed more responsible and sensitive social values when their general education in social science has been so tailored to their particular needs. Because the number of students with such personality characteristics is large and growing, this type of experimentation seems unusually important.

SUMMARY

This study has discovered no specific curricular pattern of general education, no model syllabus for a basic social science course, no pedigree of instructor and no wizardry of instructional method which should be patented for its impact on the values of students. Student values do change to some extent in college. With some students, the change is substantial. But the impetus to change does not come primarily from the formal educational process. Potency to affect student values is found in the distinctive climate of a few institutions, the individual and personal magnetism of a sensitive teacher with strong value-commitments of his own, or value-laden personal experiences of students imaginatively integrated with their intellectual development.

1

Values of American College Students

AMERICAN college students today tend to think alike, feel alike and believe alike. To an extraordinary degree, their values are the same wherever they may be studying and whatever the stage of their college careers. The great majority seem turned out of a common mold, so far as outlook on life and standards of conduct are concerned.

This phenomenon, interpreted from one point of view, shows how limited has been the overall impact of higher education on the human character with which it has worked. Evidently college in general, or colleges in particular, do not break or alter the mold of values for most students.

But the broad uniformity of student values is a baseline from which individuals do depart. To the extent that they do so—going "against the grain" as it were—they mark out the area where their education, and other factors, may have had a decisive influence.

So an understanding of the dominant pattern is the first step in appraising the specific value outcomes which may result from a student's curricular experiences.

During the last ten years, comprehensive and penetrating surveys have exposed with unusual clarity the attitudes, beliefs and aspirations of American students. They show:

First, most American students share many values in common. *There is a striking homogeneity of basic values throughout the country.*

Second, on issues where students do differ, they split in about the same proportions at most institutions. *The patterns of value tend to be similar at American colleges,* regardless of location, administration, size and background of the student body, or character of the educational program.

THE DATA

The most revealing data concerning American student values come from the following five sources:

American Council on Education, Cooperative Study of Evaluation in General Education (1)[1]

A 120-item Inventory of Beliefs was administered to students in at least 16 institutions on various occasions between 1950 and 1956. A revised form of this instrument has also been used experimentally at several institutions.

Responses on individual items have been analyzed for samples of students at Antioch, Colgate and Michigan State University.

Cornell University, Social Science Research Center (6-10)

31-page student questionnaire was administered in 1952 to 4585 students representative of the male undergraduates at 11 institutions. A similar questionnaire was given to a cross section of both male and female undergraduates at Cornell University in 1950.

Gordon W. Allport, Philip E. Vernon and Gardner V. Lindzey, *Study of Values.* (310)

This instrument has been widely used in its original and revised forms for 25 years, on a variety of student groups. A comparative analysis of published results has been specially prepared for the present report.

James M. Gillespie and Gordon W. Allport, *Youth's Outlook on the Future.* (11)

Essays written by student samples at Harvard, Radcliffe and Miami University (Ohio) in addition to student groups in other countries; supplemented by a 50-item questionnaire, "Autobiography to 2000 A.D." These have also been completed by a freshman class at Haverford College.

[1] Numbers in parentheses in the text refer to the Inventory of Data.

Ernest Havemann and Patricia West, *They Went to College.* (61)

Report on an opinion survey conducted by *Time* Magazine in 1947, of a representative cross section of 9000 American college graduates.

The data from the various surveys are remarkably consistent. Some identically worded questions and others which were similarly stated appeared on two or more of the questionnaires. The similarity of response despite the differing contexts in which they were raised warrants the conclusion that these surveys are comparable and that they can properly be used together to provide a composite view of American student values.[2]

The Common Values of American Students

The common response given by three out of four, or more, American students on these surveys, indicates that they share alike values for 1) self-confidence, 2) self-interest with a strong family tie, 3) conventional religious faith, 4) morality (with some elbow-room), 5) privatism, or a life unencumbered by public responsibilities, 6) tolerance, and 7) college. These are the pivots around which they orient their attitudes and guide their conduct.

Self-confidence

The outlook on life of most American students is contented and self-confident. They believe that:

1) everyone must determine his own destiny, and most of the important things in life are the result of a person's own efforts, rather than of circumstances beyond his control.

2) anyone can succeed by his own hard work (though one in three expects that "who you know" is also an important ingredient of getting ahead).

3) most people can be trusted.

4) their health and spirits are good and their lives will be happy and long.

At the same time, a curious, almost Malthusian fatalism characterizes students' expectations concerning the limitations of man's eco-

---

[2] The sources from which the data in this chapter are drawn are identified by the following symbols: I.B. (A.C.E. Inventory of Beliefs), C (Cornell Values Survey), A-V (Allport-Vernon Study of Values), Aut. (Autobiography to 2000 A.D.)

nomic capacities. Most students expect the "poor to be always with us."

TABLE 1: We are Masters of our Fate

On the Cornell survey, 78%-87% thought that most of the important things that happen to other people are more the result of their own efforts than of circumstances beyond their control (C #B-55).

On the Autobiography to 2000 AD, 85% of the Harvard-Radcliffe-Miami sample expected their own destiny to be determined largely by what they themselves made of it. A similar proportion of a Haverford freshmen class shared this expectation (Aut. #41).

77% on the Cornell survey agreed that "any man who is able and willing to work hard has a good chance of succeeding these days." Much the same response was given to a similar statement on the Inventory of Beliefs (#13) by students at Colgate and Michigan State.

Self-interest

Students' self-centeredness is striking. "It's only natural," most of them agree, "that a person should take advantage of every opportunity to promote his own welfare," (I.B. #39) and his first duty in our society is "to protect from harm himself and those dear to him." (I.B. #50) (also Hall, op. cit. #41) Students tend to project their self-centeredness, suspecting that most other people are likewise more inclined to look out for themselves than to help others. (A #35)

The priority which students place on themselves is confirmed by their high ranking of self-oriented values on the Allport-Vernon Study of Values. Generally an aspiration for power (identified as the "political" value), or practical, material satisfactions (the "economic" value), predominate over the "social" value (love and concern for people) or religious values. (16)

The overriding aspiration of the self-seeking American student is a "rich, full life" filled with variety, interest and perhaps excitement. He dreads monotony. Boredom would be one of the worst things many students feel could happen to them in life. (11) As they contemplate their careers, security is *not* the dominant motivation of the American student population. More students consider an opportunity to "use their talents creatively" or "to be creative and original" the most important requirement of a satisfying job. (C) Only a limited number appear driven by a competitive mania, an overwhelming

TABLE 2: Sources of Life-Satisfaction

What three things or activities in your life do you expect to give you the most satisfaction? Your career or occupation—family relationships—leisure-time, recreational activities—participation as a citizen in the affairs of your community—participation in activities directed toward national or international betterment—religious beliefs and activities. Aut. #27, C #B-46)

	Ca-reer	Fam-ily	Lei-sure	Com-munity	Nation-al, Inter-national	Re-ligion	No. of students answering
United States Harvard-Radcliffe-Miami (original) sample (on Autobiography)	83	95	60	20	17	19	756
United States Male undergraduates at 10 colleges (Cornell survey)	89	89	56	17	12	17	4451
Haverford freshmen (male)	84	89	54	11	30	17	89
Cornell (1st choice only) men	25	65	5	1	1	3	} 1066
women	8	84	2	—	—	6	
New Zealand	81	86	46	20	25	31	121
Egypt	65	60	38	48	33	49	63
Mexico	95	60	18	32	69	19	186
France	91	83	65	5	23	31	132
Italy	76	92	34	20	20	53	74
Japan	41	88	62	16	60	20	187

% of students selecting as 1st, 2d, or 3d choices:

craving for success and other marks of sheer personal ambition, though at least half consider it very important to "get ahead" in life. (Cornell A-36)

To Allport and Gillespie, American students appear radically different in these respects from the generation which completed college before the Second World War, indicating the possibility that a definite change in character has occurred. They also find that the American outlook contrasts sharply with the predominant urge of many European students to "form a character" or "become a personality" with the stress on individuality rather than on outward activity. (11)

TABLE 3: Most Important Qualification of the Ideal Job (C)

Provide an opportunity to use my special abilities or aptitudes	27%
Permit me to be creative and original	10%
Enable me to look forward to a stable, secure future	24%
Provide me with a chance to earn a good deal of money	10%
Give me an opportunity to be helpful to others	9%
Other	20%
	100%

A happy family is a vital ingredient in the American student's scheme for a full life. Seven out of ten expect their family relationships to provide them more satisfaction in life than any other activity. The proportion of women considering marriage and family of supreme importance in their lives is even higher (84%). Many of the remaining students rank family second only to their careers as a likely source of satisfaction. (C) Raising a good and happy family will be one of their proudest achievements, a large majority feel. (Aut.)

On the other hand, most American students have little time or concern for the welfare of others and their interest in social problems is extremely low.

Only one in five anticipates that a socially-oriented activity (community, national, international or religious) will be one of his three main sources of satisfaction in life, or considers helpfulness to others a highly important requirement for an ideal job. (C) (Aut.)

Even fewer would choose to devote a "windfall" or any part of one to alleviate human misery or in some way better the lot of others. (Only 3% of a Harvard-Radcliffe-Miami sample would do so.) Most would rather invest, save or spend the money for their own or their family's security or enjoyment. (11)

In a class of Haverford freshmen one in three indicated that he would be willing to make his greatest sacrifice of time, money and personal comfort to achieve an altruistic end, one in three would devote his greatest effort to secure his family's happiness and welfare, and the other would concentrate his energies on insuring his own personal happiness, success or gratifications. (Aut.) Other data indicate that the proportion of altruistically-motivated students at Haverford is unusually high compared with other American colleges. American students fell far short of students of other nationalities in their philanthropic impulses and showed less sympathetic concern for others in their personal philosophies of life. (11, 44)

Religion—but not for living

Religiousness is widespread among the contemporary American student generation. Most students express a "need to believe" and say they personally require some form of religiously-oriented philosophy of life. This is particularly the case with women; but even among male students at non-denominational colleges, 60% to 90% admit a need for religion.

TABLE 4: Need for Religion

Do you personally feel that you *need* to believe in some sort of religious faith or philosophy? (C #B-50)	78% Yes
Do you feel that you require some form of religious orientation or belief in order to achieve a fully mature philosophy of life? (Aut. #50)	
men	64% Yes
women	77% Yes

A good majority at these "secular" institutions are satisfied that their present religious faith or personal philosophy is adequate as a guide to conduct, and claim that they attend religious services with fair regularity. One in four says he attends once a week or more often, one in four does not attend at all, and the others attend frequently but not regularly. (C #B-52) After college, the attendance record improves even more. (45, 61)

Most students profess belief in the Deity either as a Supreme Being and Creator to whom they are personally accountable, or at least as a power greater than themselves, ruling the universe by natural and moral laws. At most of the non-sectarian institutions sampled, more than three out of four subscribed to a belief in God. (C #B-54) Practically no one at church-related colleges admits to atheism or agnosticism. (41) Furthermore, students are generally confident that God can and will take a hand in human affairs and see that tangible benefits accrue to the righteous. "No task is too great or too difficult when we know that God is on our side," they agree. (I.B. #78) Especially when they enter college, students believe that "if a person is honest, works hard and trusts in God, he will reap material as well as spiritual rewards." (I.B. #119)

The Cornell study found that most students attach great importance to a basic faith in man as good, and that this faith cuts across all specific values. Their religious-ethical system is an integral part of this faith.

Yet their value-systems will not stand up when undercut by forced choices between alternatives which involve conflicting values. Nor does religion appear to be a vital concern of most students. Few students relate the practical course of everyday living with their religious beliefs. Only a small minority expect religious activities to provide one of their main sources of satisfaction in life. (see above, Table 3) They tend to place more faith in secular, material forces than in spiritual power as the real determinants of human events. More students, for instance, consider that the United States should rely on military power to prevent war than would be willing to trust to individual spiritual values and inner resources for this purpose. (47% as against 33% on the Cornell survey [C #B-57])

A real hiatus separates religious interest and social responsibility. Few students seem to recognize social or humanitarian implications in their religious faith. Firm belief in God does not seem to diminish prejudice toward people of other races. Indeed, strong religious belief tends to be associated with racial and ethnic prejudice. (51) Students' religion does not usually increase their willingness to accept others if it involves some expense to themselves. Nor does it lead them to become personally active in the promotion of justice in human relations. The devout are no more sympathetic than others toward public action to advance human welfare. Actually the *less* religious tend to be the more humanitarian, and the more concerned about social injustices and misery. "As one moves away from the concept of an all-powerful and all-wise God one finds greater acceptance of the practical application of the concept of the brotherhood of man," concludes the major study of the religious beliefs of youth. (45)[3]

There are to be sure some "islands" of students with religious convictions which are profound. In these instances their responses indicate that their religion not only governs their personal lives but guides them to sensitive human relations and social responsibilities.

But in Gordon Allport's observation, "the task of integrating the values of a religion with the present needs of daily life is one that very few youths seem able to carry through. . . . In most instances one sees only a scramble for tangible types of safety in a menacing world where catastrophic change is under way. For the majority of youth religion in large part seems like a remote if pleasant memory. What it teaches is unclear and its bearing on present activities is dim. To borrow Renan's phrase its nostalgic quality is like the perfume of an empty vase." (45)

Morality—with elbow room

A strong tendency towards orthodoxy characterizes students' ethical systems, despite the "boldness" of college talk, dress and outward social conduct. They are clear that right is different from wrong, and that conscience provides man an inherent guide to know the distinction. (I.B. #9) In personal practice and fundamental belief, students generally hold to moral standards which are thoroughly conventional. Honesty, reliability, decency, unselfishness and integrity are highly valued. (11) So, to a very large extent, is personal restraint in sexual relations.

Two specific studies point up the prevailing student code of sex morality:

[3] Although this study by Ross concerned principally youth who were members of YMCA's, a similar conclusion regarding the failure of religious belief to carry over to humanitarianism was also reached in earlier studies by Ferguson and Kirkpatrick. (39, 42) One must exempt those of Jewish faith from most of these observations, however. They tend far more than Protestants or Catholics to be sympathetic to a welfare philosophy of government, opposed to the suppression of civil liberties, and genuinely concerned about issues of social justice. (See (45); also Cornell Values Survey.)

At Chicago, an intimate discussion of moral issues with a group of freshman women showed that a large majority subscribed to standards they said represented those of their parents in regard to sex relations and other ethical questions, and that they fully expected to maintain these standards. Furthermore, the actual opinions and behavior of the girls were more orthodox than was attributed to them by their fellow-students, suggesting that talk may be more "libertarian" at a place like Chicago than practice.[4]

At Cornell, in the values survey, students by and large took no hard and fast stand on moral questions, especially in judging the conduct of others. They attached little importance to chastity as a criterion for choosing a mate (less than 5% would break an engagement on the ground that the fiance had pre-marital relations). Yet few of them would justify a life of promiscuity—either for men or women—and most evidently found the canons of chastity appropriate to govern their personal lives. The idea of a double standard, with greater freedom to be enjoyed by men than women, carried no weight with either, though men tended to be more broad-minded in general about the subject of sex. An analysis by the Social Science Research Center concluded that about one fourth of the students were consistently permissive in their views, one in ten consistently restrictive and the rest in between.[5]

Apparently many students are inclined to tolerate behavior on the part of others which they would not approve for themselves. Very few are prepared to be social censors. Most consider moral standards a personal matter, immune from outside inspection or criticism. Permissiveness in regard to the conduct of others is as much a part of the American student's moral outlook as is the orthodoxy of his own code. Thus within the college, or rather the student community, no social sanctions attach to violations of the standards accepted by the majority. Freedom to deviate if an individual wishes is fully acknowledged.

There is further indication that the conventional moral code may not have an all-encompassing grip on American student conduct.

[4] Unpublished M. A. thesis for the University of Chicago Divinity School by Marjorie Ann Diederick.
[5] Cornell University Social Science Research Center, "The Student Thinks About Love and Marriage," an unpublished manuscript; also Rose K. Goldsen, Report on the Cornell Student Body, op. cit. no. 9.

Moral values are not uppermost in the priority scale of many students. Though real enough in themselves, they do not necessarily overrule other values in case of conflict. When Haverford freshmen contemplated the worst things that might justifiably be said about them during their lifetime, more were worried about the possibility of failure in personal achievement than were concerned about their moral reputation. If in a concrete situation being unselfish or telling the truth would interfere with success and advancement in one's work, which value would prevail? For a large number of students, if the Haverford freshman is representative, the latter might well win out. As a matter of fact, the wide respect professed for unselfishness appears utterly incompatible with the extraordinary devotion previously noted to purely self-interest. Perhaps it is the bad social *reputation* of selfishness and egotism which bothers the American student, rather than a sense of its intrinsic wrongfulness.

TABLE 5: What Makes For a Bad Reputation—
A Haverford Freshman Estimate

Content analysis of the replies of a Haverford College freshman class to the question: "What are the two worst things that could justifiably be said about you during your entire lifetime?" (Aut. #40)

	% of students noting this characteristic	% of total qualities mentioned	
Personal failure			
in work and use of talents	25	19)	
in drive and "success" attributes	17	13)	42
in family relations	14	10)	
Moral failure			
selfishness	24	18)	
other egotistical qualities	12	9)	38
lack of standard moral virtues	15	11)	
(honesty, sexual propriety etc.)			
Civic failure			
performance (not being a good citizen)	11	8)	
attitudes ("reactionary,"		)	14
"prejudiced")	8	6)	
Social failure			
(lack of respectability, being a "fruit")	8		6
No answer	15		

The chinks in the moral armor of American students are most obvious in regard to cheating. On this issue, the situation varies greatly among institutions as will appear in later discussion. But the practice is so widespread as to challenge the well-nigh universal claim of students that they value honesty as a moral virtue. Frequent cheating is admitted by 40% or more at a large number of colleges, often with no apology or sense of wrong-doing.

No really adequate explanation of the paradox has yet appeared, but a study at Harvard sheds some light, indicating that such values as self-advancement, personal friendship and holding the respect of one's fellow students often conflict with and override the value of honesty, at least in academic matters. (307) Students were asked what they would do if as a proctor of an examination they detected a fellow-student cheating. Readiness to discharge their academic responsibility (and hence fully maintain the standard of honesty) depended first on whether the culprit was a personal friend, second, on whether their failure to report would become known to university authorities, and third, on what they thought other students would think of them if they did or did not make a report. Practically no one would have upheld the honesty code regardless of all of these considerations. What is more, self-interest seems to have been a more influential factor in determining what to do than either friendship or the prevailing view of proper conduct among the student community. In other words, the decision of a great many students hinged in the last analysis on whether their own standing with the authorities would be jeopardized.

This implies that American students tend to value self-interest first, then social acceptance, friendship, and moral principles in that order, when they are in conflict. The Cornell Values Survey confirms the conclusion that by and large the religious-ethical systems of American students are not firm enough to resist undercutting by competing value standards.

TABLE 6: The Undercutting of Moral Values

Based on data from Samuel A. Stouffer, "Analysis of Conflicting Social Norms," *American Sociological Review*, December, 1949.
Undercutting of honesty by personal friendship:
66% would not report the cheater if he were a personal friend; only

16% would fail to report him if he were not a friend—assuming no public knowledge of the incident.

68% favored strong punitive action in the case of cheater who was not friend; only 16% favored such action when the individual involved was a friend.

The factor of friendship by itself thus altered the attitude of about 50% of the students.

Undercutting of honesty by social pressure:

Only 5% chose a course of conduct which they felt would conflict with what most of their fellow students approved, when the cheater was not a friend; virtually no one would conflict with the social norm in the case of a friend—again assuming no public knowledge of the incident.

The great majority considered that their fellow-students would approve a course of extreme leniency for a friend, and a more punitive one for someone who was not. Social pressure reinforced the personal value for friendship as against an absolute standard of honesty and also against the assumed standards held by the institution.

Undercutting of friendship by self-interest:

Assuming that the incident would be known, regardless of the proctor's action, a large number of students changed their stand. Only 27% (rather than 66%) would fail to report their friend; 40% (instead of 16%) would support strong punitive action against him. Less than 40% would stick by their friend in a way they felt the authorities would disapprove, assuming they would be found out. Thus about 2 out of 5 would let honesty overrule friendship, *if* there were a danger of being caught and having to pay the consequences.

"Privatism"

Most American students desire to separate themselves from their political and social context. They shun civic responsibilities and have little personal interest in public affairs.

Only 3% gave top priority in considering their plans for the future to being active in national affairs or being a useful citizen, in marked contrast to the outlook of students of several other nationalities. (11)

Only 17% expected that participating as a citizen in the affairs of the community would be one of *three* activities giving them the most satisfaction in life.

Only 12% expect activity directed toward national or international betterment would be among the three most satisfying. (C)

Furthermore, a reputation for failure in the tasks of citizenship does not seem to bother many students. (see Table 5, above)

This lack of personal concern for a civic or public role also emerges when students evaluate the importance of various educational goals. On the Cornell survey half consider the development of knowledge and interest in community and world problems *an* important goal of a university. But fewer than 3% ranked this of first importance compared with such goals as vocational training, developing an ability to get along with different kinds of people, providing a basic general education or helping to develop moral capacities. Five times as many students chose as a university's most important function the development of students' ability to get along with people as picked the goal of citizenship participation.

American students exhibit a bland belief in the political process of popular democracy, but shy away from personal political participation. For instance, they state they do not consider writing congressmen or public officials a waste of time, but very few bother to do it. While the great majority do vote when they can qualify by age, only a small minority take a really active part in politics. The *Time* survey found that even among college graduates, no more than 20% could be considered politically active to the extent that they campaigned, contributed money, or communicated their views on policy to a public official or representative. (34) The percentage of current students really interested in politics is even smaller. (35, 36) Apathy is particularly pronounced in regard to local government and politics.

The casualness of most students about politics is reflected in the poverty of their information about important political events, procedures and personalities. They rarely understand how political parties function, the significance of primary elections, the duties of major agencies of American government, or the critical issues of domestic or foreign policy. It is the exception when a student can identify the Premier of Russia, the Secretary of State or any other Cabinet officer in the United States government, or the governor of his own state. A student hardly ever knows who is his precinct committeeman, ward leader, representative in the state legislature, congressman or either United States Senator from his state. (31, 35, 36, 37)

There is a real question whether the value attached by American students to the rituals of the democratic political process—such as voting and writing one's governmental representatives—is grounded

TABLE 7: A Belief in Popular Democracy?

	% agreeing students at various institutions	college graduates
1. The weight of public opinion:		
There's little use writing to public officials because often they aren't really interested in the problems of the average man. (C #C-63)	20-36	
Sending letters to Congressmen has little influence on legislation. (I. B. #24 *Time*)	12-27	24
2. The value of voting:		
In some elections there is not much point in voting because the outcome is fairly certain. (I. B. #57 *Time*)	11-16	10
3. Party control:		
Political parties are run by insiders who are not concerned with the public welfare. (I. B. #107 *Time*)	25-47	20
Political candidates are usually run by political machines. (C #C-2)	18-37	
4. Governmental integrity and responsibility:		
Public officials may try to be honest but they are caught in a web of influence which tends to corrupt them. (I. B. #83)	45-77	
The government is more interested in winning elections than in the welfare of the people. (I. B. #48)	14-49	
5. Political competence of the public:		
When the public is really concerned about an issue, its judgment is usually correct and unassailable, no matter how complex the issue. (C #C-1)	41-56	
The public judgment is usually correct if concerned. (*Time*)		62 *disagree*

firmly in democratic belief. There is *no* uniformity of conviction in regard to the capacity of people to govern themselves, or in the efficacy of representative democracy to produce either wise government or disinterested and responsible government. (See Table 7) As a matter of fact, about as many students take a cynical or "realist" view as accept the democratic credo on such matters as the incompetence of the general public to decide complex issues, and the perversion of government and politics to selfish ends by influence and machine control. This discrepancy between idealistic assumptions about American politics and actual practice may account for the failure of students to take any profound interest in political action. They may doubt that their efforts could result in any good. On the other hand, the idealists appear no more concerned than the cynics to exercise their citizen rights in the steering of public policy. There is no evidence of a connection between belief in the ideology of democracy and a disposition to apply it in political practice. While political cynicism may not be the predominant mood on the campus, political indifference surely is.

In trying to account for the phenomenon of privatism among American students a group of 300 Harvard and Radcliffe students came up with the following reasons: 1) United States security from invasion, 2) pressures toward success (defined as a rich and full personal life), 3) the opprobrium attached to politics and public service, 4) the prolonged period of adolescence leading to civic irresponsibility and disinterest, 5) emphasis on rights rather than duties of democracy, and 6) discouragement regarding the possibility of being personally effective on political and international issues. (11) Viewed in the total perspective of the value profile, the second of these reasons seems most pertinent. A self-oriented life has little room in it for outpourings of social consciousness and civic-mindedness. Nor do most students find political power an objective worth disturbing their personal privacy and contented family life.

This impression is supported by analysis of the motivation of students toward the performance of public duties such as military service. The overwhelming majority fully expect to serve if drafted, but feel no compunction to enlist and no sense of guilt about being deferred for college while others of their age are called up. Very few look on the prospect of military service with a sense of patriotic de-

TABLE 8: Internationalism

As a solution to the problem of international relations, favor a world government, worked out perhaps through an extension of the United Nations (in preference to other alternatives such as strong nationalism, regionalism or federal union of non-communist countries). (Aut. #46)	62-78% agree
The United Nations should have the right to make decisions which would bind members to a course of action. (*Time*)	78% agree (college graduates)
More power should be given the United Nations. (Turner, op. cit. no 37)	70% agree
No world organization should have the right to tell Americans what they can or cannot do. (I. B. #96) at college entrance later in college	53-69% } disagree 77-82% }
Which do you personally count on as the more effective deterrent against war: the atom bomb or the U. N.? (C #B-67)	50% atom bomb
It is highly important for the U. S. to rely on military power if we are to prevent another war. (C #B-57)	47% agree
The best assurance of peace is for the United States to have the strongest army, navy, air force, and the most atom bombs. (I. B. #102)	29-41% agree
Lowering tarriffs to admit more foreign goods into this country lowers our standard of living. (I. B. #3, *Time*) at college entrance later in college college graduates	47-60% disagree 73-78% " 65% "
If we allow more immigrants into this country we will lower our standards of culture. (I. B. #43, *Time*) at college entrance later in college college graduates	70-73% disagree 74-82% " 69% "

votion. During the Korean war a majority of students subscribed to the prevailing idealistic interpretation that "we are fighting today for . . . . the free peoples of the world against dictatorship" and averred that they owed it to their government to protect it in return for more important privileges. (C #C-30, #C-46) But at bottom, the degree of their willingness to serve depended not so much on ideological convictions or patriotic commitment, as on personal factors. Just how seriously would service uproot well-laid educational and vocational plans or jeopardize family security or postpone marriage? These were the vital considerations for most students. (6, 7, 8)

The surface character of students' political idealism also appears in their attitudes towards international affairs. By the time they graduate, about three-fourths of the students across the country qualify as "internationalists." They declare they are willing to have a world organization make binding decisions on national governments, including their own. They dismiss the high tariff rationale. They see no great dangers in immigration. (See Table 8) But these questions of international policy do not deeply concern them. Few students intend to devote much of their time or energy to influencing the course of world events one way or the other. (See Table 3 above) Even though they consider another major war a likely occurrence in the next generation (C #B-57, Aut. #42) this is not sensed as a sufficiently personal threat to galvanize strenuous action to avert it. For instance, only one in seven of a class of Haverford freshmen indicated that he would be prepared to make the greatest sacrifice of personal comfort, time and money to achieve a world at peace; yet a larger proportion of the Haverford students gave evidence of concern about international affairs than at any other institution studied. Furthermore, fully as many students would place primary confidence for security and peace in national military power as in international organization. (C #B-57, #B-67)

Tolerance

American students now display relatively little prejudice towards people of different color and nationality. Their easy personal tolerance carries over to convinced support for a broad range of civil rights for minority groups. It has become a hallmark of the college-educated today to believe in equality as an inescapable feature of the harmonious society they expect to inhabit. They oppose discrimination against minority groups in almost any form. On the other hand, they divide almost 50-50 on whether equality should be governmentally induced and enforced.

A minority, especially strong among Southern white students, still upholds the color bar. Pockets of intolerance also persist towards other groups—foreigners, Jews, and radicals of various hues. A surprisingly large number of students when they first enter college con-

TABLE 9: Prejudice and Tolerance: Racial

Generally speaking, Negroes are lazy and ignorant. (C #C-9)	14% or less accept this view at ten institutions surveyed, except Yale (21%), Texas (31%), North Carolina (44%)
Most Negroes would become overbearing and disagreeable if not kept in their place. (I. B. #68)	73-91% disagree
Manual labor and unskilled jobs seem to fit the Negro mentality and ability better than more skilled or responsible work. (I. B. #81)	75-92% disagree
Negroes have their rights, but it is best to keep them in their own districts and schools and to prevent too much contact with whites. (I. B. #109)	69-93% disagree
It is not true that children of minority groups or other races should play among themselves. (Time)	86% agree (graduates)
Would you like to see greater equality between white and colored races within your lifetime? (Aut. #47)	83-93% agree
All Americans—Negroes, Jews, the foreign-born and others—should have equal opportunity in social, economic and political affairs. (Time)	80% agree (graduates)
The Federal Government should require all employers to hire people without regard to their race, religion, color or nationality. (C #C7)	44-62% agree at the ten institutions surveyed except for Texas (34%) and North Carolina (26%)

sider foreign "agitators" have menaced real Americanism, though many change to a less prejudiced view later on. Most students, however, have gone a long way toward dismantling the barriers of personal prejudice which have encumbered the flow of human relationships and are ready to live and let live regardless of the idiosyncracies of those who are "different."

TABLE 10: Prejudice and Tolerance: Ethnic

This country would be better off if there were not so many foreigners here. (C #C-10)	10% or less agreed at the ten institutions surveyed, except at North Carolina (20%)
Foreigners usually have peculiar and annoying habits. (I. B. #100, *Time*)	72-90% disagreed (students) 68% disagreed (graduates)
The worst danger to real Americanism during the last 50 years has come from foreign ideas and agitators. (I. B. #90)	49-69% disagreed (students) 53% disagreed (graduates)

College

Students' valuation of the *importance of college education* is very high (though for different reasons). They also think well of almost all aspects of college life, including their teachers. As a rule, three out of four consider what they are learning is "very worthwhile." Less than one in five thinks college does not equip them for life outside the campus. The great majority reject out of hand the charge that college education does more to break down values than to build up ideals, though a fairly substantial minority at some institutions believe more emphasis should be placed on teaching religious, and especially American ideals and values. Students at most institutions widely defend faculty members against charges of radicalism and atheism and general lack of respect for religious values. Relatively few see a need for more teachers with conservative views on their campus.

Students are not entirely uncritical about college. As a matter of fact student bodies vary considerably in the degree of their appreciation of college (a point to be discussed later). What disturbs a fair number is "production-line teaching methods," and only one in three appears satisfied with the job that his particular college is doing to fulfill the educational goals he considers important.

Nevertheless, on an overall appraisal, most college graduates cherish the education they have had, and if they had it to do over again would choose to repeat the course of study they took and at the same campus from which they graduated. (61)

TABLE 11: Appreciation of College

	percentage of students who agree at ten institutions in Cornell survey
College does not really equip you for life outside the campus. (C #D-17)	18
Most of what I am learning in college is very worthwhile. (C #D-18)	71
College education does more to break down values than to build up ideals. (C #D-23)	15
American colleges today should place more emphasis on teaching religious values. (C #D-20)	22
American colleges today should place more emphasis on teaching American ideals and values. (C #D-22)	31
Too many college teachers lack respect for religious values. (C #D-26)	17
Charges of atheism among faculty members are justified. (C #B-39)	14
Charges of radicalism among faculty members are justified. (C #B-39)	20
Would like to see more teachers with conservative views on my campus. (C #D-25)	11
Charges of "production-line" teaching methods are justified. (C #B-39)	51
My own university is doing a very good job, in general, in fulfilling the educational goals I consider important. (C #B-17)	33

The student's respect for education and the college faculty as he knows them is evidenced in his stand on the touchy issue of academic freedom. Despite the strong repressive pressures during the heyday of McCarthyism, students by and large appear to have maintained a firm belief in the right of a teacher to teach his subject, regardless of his past or present political views and affiliations. Surveys of student opinion on academic freedom at such "exposed" institutions as UCLA, the University of California at Berkeley and Columbia found "the right of an instructor to believe what he wishes and to continue to teach in his field of competence is affirmed by a very special kind of authority—those toward whom his teaching efforts are directed." At Columbia, students overwhelmingly condemned congressional investigation of colleges in principle and as currently practiced. At all three institutions a majority of students were found to have no categorical objection to the employment of Communists on the faculty, a quite extreme test, under the circumstances, of their devotion to the principle of academic freedom. (59)

ISSUES WHICH DIVIDE

The value profile of American students shows some deep divisions among them as well as the great uniformities of outlook just discussed. Some of these differences of opinion, belief and standards appear to reflect prevailing social and ideological cleavages and the diversified philosophies of life in American society.

For instance, students are split the country over regardless of the character and location of their colleges on such issues as: 1) the importance of discipline and authority in raising a family, 2) the importance of government action to foster economic and social well-being, 3) the importance of military power in maintaining peace and national security, 4) the importance of insuring political conformity and restraining radicalism.

Order in the family

American students are not of one mind as to how children should be brought up. Actually many of them seem to have no mind on the subject or at least are very confused. Quite a large number are inclined to feel parents should practice more discipline, and that children should learn obedience. 44% on the Cornell survey felt parents aren't strict enough with their children. But obviously many disagree, and permissiveness in family relations apparently grows in favor as students progress through their college careers. Furthermore, only a negligible few would defend the teaching of unquestioning obedience.

(C #C-52) But an overwhelming majority count on father to exercise a kind of reserve authority and as head of the family to tell the others at times what they can and cannot do. (I.B. #2) Strongly devoted as they are to the family as a central point of reference in their lives, American students have no common conception of what a family really is and how it should function.

Government—little or much?

Students do not agree on a philosophy of government, especially in regard to its relation to business and the economic order. The majority are clearly conservative in the sense that they have a strong commitment to "free enterprise" and are suspicious about the activities of a "welfare state." On matters involving controversy between business and labor two to one will normally be anti-labor. There is almost a total absence of anything that might be called political radicalism. But a sizeable group are New Dealers and their number is growing. Among younger college graduates, the division is just about 50-50, according to the criteria used in the *Time* survey in 1947. The lines between conservative and liberal are not clear and sharp, however, because most students do not seem to have worked out a coherent and well-defined political ideology. They can express views which seem to put them in different camps, but one gets the feeling that the roots are shallow. Issues which struck home hard in the 30's, both in the country at large and with students, now have less significance. Political realities have changed and governmental powers, which were formerly a subject of controversy, are now taken for granted. It is symptomatic that despite the tendency of students to lean towards economic conservatism and a "business" outlook towards government, only one in three now takes the position that "the best government is one which governs least," or that government planning will destroy essential freedom.

Significantly, the economic status of a student has little to do with his economic and political philosophy (except possibly in regard to his attitude towards business and labor relations). As likely as not, a conservative's family may have been scraping along on a low income, and a liberal's to have had a Long Island estate. On the other hand the conservative *is* likely to be a Republican. And Jewish students are much *less* likely than Protestants or Catholics to be devoted to laissez-faire or to damn the welfare state.

TABLE 12: The Business of Government

	% agreeing	
	Students	Graduates
Democracy depends fundamentally on the existence of free business enterprise. (C #C-25) (*Time*)	62	72
The "welfare state" tends to destroy individual initiative. (C #C-29)	60	
The best government is the one which governs least. (C #C-24) (*Time*) (I. B. #52)		
Average of all colleges		
(Cornell)	31	
Colgate and Michigan State		
(I. B.)	35-45	52
Government planning almost inevitably results in the loss of essential liberties and freedom. (C #C-28)	31	
Individual liberty and justice is not possible in socialist countries. (*Time*)		46
Government planning should be strictly limited. (*Time*)		51

The power of the sword

Students are really confused when they come to evaluate the role of power in international affairs. About half are power-oriented in the sense that they think that military power (in the hands of the United States) is an important deterrent against war. (C #B-57 and B-67, I. B. #102) (See Table 8, above.) Two out of three idealized the Korean war as a fight to defend freedom the world over. (C #C-30) Two out of three consider it a duty to bear arms to protect their government. (C #C-46) Yet students, two to one, condemn war as morally wrong. (C #C-39)

Putting these disparate views together, it appears that approximately one-third of American students rather definitely shun war and military power as necessary or worthy instruments of policy in the world today (though far fewer would go the limit of conscientiously objecting to war and military service). Another third evidently have no compunctions at all about the use of power on either pragmatic or moral grounds. The remaining third seem to have qualms about wars' immorality but justify reliance on military power to fulfill idealistic ends and maybe prevent war itself. The absence of a settled "philosophy" is the dominant impression given by most students in all three groups. What they are expressing is an off-hand feeling about matters under public discussion rather than a considered value-judgment based on solid conviction. There is thus little evidence of firmness about the state of the student mind toward this major issue of the world's future.

The danger of dissidence

Students have not been immune from the raging controversy over the proper treatment of political non-conformists and the measures necessary to defend the country against subversion in a period of cold war. They are divided over the dangers to be feared and the degree of repression of civil liberties justified. But the majority maintain a fairly firm commitment to civil rights and the commitment tends to become stronger the longer students have been at college. (60)

About two out of five, however, would hold a pretty tight rein on persons whose political or economic views made their loyalty suspect. It would certainly be unwise, these students believe, to let such people have a chance to be elected to public office. Radicals among teachers should be watched. The Communist Party should be outlawed. Conscientious objectors should leave the country. At some institutions, especially in the South, the proportion of students favoring repressive action is notably higher than at others.

It is characteristic of those who would justify suppressing civil liberties in concrete situations that they continue to proclaim devotion to the abstract principles of the Bill of Rights. Almost all the "repressive" students affirm that freedom of religion, a jury trial, the right to move, the right to vote, the right to have a public hearing and freedom of expression are highly important for a government to respect and maintain. For instance, in the Cornell student body, 88% of those who favored suppressing "unwholesome religions" considered the unrestricted right to practice religion of "highest" importance; 82% of those who would keep people from spreading dangerous ideas thought freedom of speech was extremely important. (C)

TABLE 13: Nonconformity and Civil Liberty

	Percentage of students agreeing
It's unwise to give people with dangerous social and economic viewpoints a chance to be elected. (C #C-3) average of all colleges surveyed	41
Texas	53
Harvard	25
Steps should be taken right away to outlaw the Communist Party. (C #C-27) all colleges	35
Texas	55
Harvard	22
If you refuse to support your government in a war you shouldn't continue to live in a country. (C #C-50) all colleges	32
Texas	42
Harvard	26
A lot of teachers, these days, have radical ideas which need to be carefully watched. (I. B. #66) Michigan State (freshmen	59
(upperclassmen	50
Colgate (freshmen	47
(sophomores	17

This then is a composite profile of American student values today. The broad features are remarkably alike. But the discriminating eye can also discern the distinguishing traits of a "liberal" and a "conservative" group, the progressive and the traditionalist, the permissive and the compulsive.

2

Value-outcomes of a College Education

W<small>HAT</small> happens to the values of American students when they go to college? How different are the outlook and standards of behavior of the man or woman who has been "higher-educated"? Does the experience seem to change in any significant way the beliefs and the character which a freshman brings with him when he enrolls?

The overall conclusion of this study is that college does make a difference—but not a very fundamental one for most students. Basic values remain largely constant through college.

The changes which do occur bring greater consistency into the value-patterns of the students and fit these patterns to a well-established standard of what a college graduate in American society is expected to believe and do. But the college student is not front-runner in a broad forward movement of values within the culture at large. If anything the "typical" college graduate is a cultural rubber-stamp for the social heritage as it stands rather than the instigator of new patterns of thought and new standards of conduct.

College socializes, but does not really liberalize the student.

These generalizations do not hold for all students and all colleges. There are wide differences both among and within institutions. The point made by a leading authority on psychological studies of values is well-taken that the exact role of colleges in value development remains undefined. (105)

The Changes Which College Makes

Three bodies of evidence indicate something of the scope and character of the changes which occur in the values held by college students. First, the attitudes of college graduates have been contrasted with those held by the general population on a number of issues. Second, the beliefs and opinions of freshmen have been compared with those of upperclassmen and alumni at several institutions. Third, some "longitudinal" studies have been conducted, showing the differences in outlook of the same individuals at various stages of their education. The principal material on which this report has drawn is presented in the Inventory of Data, Section II.

From Diversity to Uniformity—Acquiring the College Outlook

Seniors as they emerge from college are far more in agreement among themselves on many issues than when they entered. They have given up extreme views, or at least views which set them apart from the "normal" upperclassman at their institution.

This uniformity of outlook among seniors is so pronounced that one can even design a scale which aptly indicates how much any particular student is like a senior at his college. For instance an intensive study of the intellectual and personality development of students at Vassar (89) revealed some 150 traits which were significantly characteristic of seniors but not of freshmen. Combined, these constituted a "Vassar Developmental Scale" which has been statistically validated.[1]

Among value judgments more typical of seniors than of freshmen at Vassar are:

Freedom from compulsiveness:
The senior, compared with the freshman, would rather be a brilliant but unstable worker than a steady and dependable one, doesn't particularly care how people dress, or feel the need to plan far ahead.

Tolerant, impunitive attitudes toward others:
The senior is not so critical as the freshman of persons who become intoxicated, who don't vote, who have intercourse before marriage,

[1] The total scale was found to have a reliability of .84 (KR-20)

are lawbreakers, or don't take things seriously enough. She tends not to set arbitrary standards of right and wrong conduct, and judge others by them.

Critical attitudes toward parents and family:
The senior is more independent of her family, critical of its habits, under less sense of obligation.

Critical or rebellious attitudes toward the state, laws, rules etc.:
The senior more often than the freshman justifies the breaking of rules on occasion, including civil disobedience; questions whether "communism is the most hateful thing in the world today" or whether the American way of life should be preserved unchanged; would prefer to betray country rather than best friend.

Religious liberalism:
The senior goes to church and prays less than the freshman, and is less likely to believe in the second coming of Christ, a life hereafter and even that there is a God.

Unconventionality:
The senior is more likely than the freshman to admit to conduct and attitudes contrary to conventional moral taboos concerning drinking, telling the truth, sexual propriety, and even theft. She feels people would be happier if sex experience before marriage were taken for granted in both men and women, and that in illegitimate pregnancies abortion is in many cases the most reasonable alternative. She thinks she would probably get into a movie without paying if sure she would not be seen.

These particular views, it should be emphasized, are not unanimously shared by the Vassar seniors, nor would they necessarily be representative of college seniors everywhere. But they do indicate what is apparently the lodestone towards which the values of girls coming to Vassar are attracted. Students tended to shed divergent attitudes which they may have brought with them as they became "seniorized."

A study of changing beliefs at Antioch, Colgate and Michigan State illustrates the same process, with the principal readjustment apparently taking place during the first two years. (70, 280, 287) In the first two institutions the Inventory of Beliefs (ACE Cooperative Study) was taken by freshmen when they entered and retaken by the same students later (at the end of the freshman year at Antioch, and the end of the sophomore year at Colgate). At Michigan State, the Inventory was given simultaneously to freshmen and to a sample of upperclassmen. The results show that in each case there was much more agreement on the various items among the students when they had been at college some time than when they just arrived. Most freshmen tended 1) to keep their views if they coincided with the prevailing sentiment of upperclassmen, 2) to change their views if they did not so coincide. The net result was to encourage greater uniformity of outlook as the students progressed through college.

In general these attitudinal changes resulted at the institutions concerned in a well-defined upperclass "model" of beliefs which emphasized (a) a free market place for ideas, based on respect for intelligence and acceptance of a wide diversity of opinions and beliefs, (b) a free melting pot of peoples and cultures, rejecting racial and ethnic stereotypes and discriminatory social barriers, (c) a self-critical approach to the national American culture based on a recognition of world interdependence and rejection of chauvinism, (d) a tolerance of unconventional behavior in social relations and a less repressive attitude toward moral taboos, (e) skepticism of the supernatural as a determining force in human affairs.

TABLE 14: Student Values—Upperclass Model

(Freshman diversity vs. upperclass uniformity on selected items from the Inventory of Beliefs)

	Antioch		Colgate		Michigan State	
Percentage who rejected the following beliefs at:	Freshmen		Fresh	Soph	Fresh	Upperclass
	At entrance	At end of year				
a) *Freedom of thought*						
We are finding out today that liberals really are softheaded, gullible and potentially dangerous					67	83
Being a successful wife and mother is more a matter of instinct than of training	58	81				

TABLE 14: Student Values—Upperclass Model—*Continued*

Percentage who rejected the following beliefs at:	Antioch Freshmen		Colgate		Michigan State	
	At entrance	At end of year	Fresh	Soph	Fresh	Upperclass
Modern paintings look like something dreamed up in a horrible nightmare			58	83		
Ministers who preach socialistic ideas are a disgrace to the church			63	81	55	79
A lot of teachers, these days, have radical ideas which need to be carefully watched			53	83		
b) Racial tolerance						
One trouble with Jewish businessmen is that they stick together and prevent other people from having a fair chance in competition			63	79	64	78
There may be a few exceptions, but in general Jews are pretty much alike			64	79	59	78
c) Rejecting ethnocentrism						
Anything we do for a good cause is justified	67	80			41	76
Voting determines whether or not a country is democratic					52	89
Americans may tend to be materialistic, but at least they aren't cynical and decadent like most Europeans	68	81	54	79	51	68
Europeans criticize the United States for its materialism but such criticism is only to cover up their realization that American culture is far superior to their own	77	87	67	91	50	78

TABLE 14: Student Values—Upperclass Model—*Continued*

Percentage who rejected the following beliefs at:	Antioch		Colgate		Michigan State	
	Freshmen		Fresh	Soph	Fresh	Upperclass
	At entrance	At end of year				
No world organization should have the right to tell Americans what they can or cannot do			69	77	53	82
d) *Moral permissiveness*						
Books and movies should start dealing with entertaining or uplifting themes instead of the present unpleasant, immoral or tragic ones	57	80				
Literature should not question the basic moral concepts of society					63	78
Our rising divorce rate is a sign that we should return to the values which our grandparents held			55	77	47	74
People who say they're religious but don't go to church are just hypocrites	74	91	65	82		
A sexual pervert is an insult to humanity and should be punished severely	72	87	60	88	49	79
e) *Skepticism of the supernatural*						
Miracles have always taken place whenever the need for them has been great enough			61	80	47	69

It is apparent that in most respects a majority of the freshmen were already inclined to accept this model, so that the person who did not was out of step not only with the upperclassmen but with the preponderant sentiment of his classmates as well. To maintain his idiosyncracy against these twin pressures, plus whatever influence in the same direction might come from his instruction would require a sturdy character indeed, or extremely strong countervailing forces from family or other sources. As a matter of fact, most students (at least those that did not drop out) did make the adjustment.

The classic demonstration of the phenomenon of adaptation to a college norm is Newcomb's prewar study of the transformation of attitudes of Bennington College girls. (85) He found that most of these students took on, in greater or less degree, the pattern of values acknowledged in the college community even though it fundamentally opposed (especially in its "radical" approach to economic and social questions) the basic assumptions with which they had grown up in a family environment of wealth and economic power. The mark of a student leader usually was his championship of the outlook and values of the community. He was "like his class, only more so." Of course Bennington's model was quite unrepresentative of college values generally, but the process of change which went on is probably similar to what happens elsewhere.

Towards Flexibility and Sociability

If the thesis just suggested is sound, one would expect that most of the changes in student values would tend in the direction of the overall profile set forth in the previous chapter, unless certain special personality, institutional or other influences intervened. Students who at first differed from the common values prevailing among students would come to accept them more and more. But on issues which divided the general student population, the division would be perpetuated as the student took sides with those who espoused the values he brought with him to college.

The evidence reviewed largely confirms this expectation. The movement of values during college is generally along the lines witnessed at Vassar, Colgate, and Michigan State. Students become somewhat less rigid, dogmatic and absolute in the standards and beliefs they hold, more critical of authority *per se*, more self-confident and self-reliant, also more self-centered, less prejudiced towards people of different races and more tolerant of those who do not conform to traditional mores.

Students become less dogmatic

Total scores made on the Inventory of Beliefs, which gauge the overall acceptance of "authoritarian" stereotypes and clichés, show that students tend to reject such concepts more at the end of college than when they entered. There is some variation among institutions in the amount of change recorded, and in few cases is the average change for an entire student body breathtaking. But the trend is clearly and customarily towards increased flexibility of belief. Change is usually greatest with students who start with the most rigid attitudes. (1)

The most important significance of the changes recorded is not the modification of attitudes on particular issues but the increased tendency of students to reject dogmatism *per se*. It is apparent that students often accept or disagree with certain of the items because

TABLE 15: Changes in Student Dogmatism During College[2]

College	Pre-test	Post-test	Difference
1	75.9	87.1	11.2
5	59.0	70.0	11.0
6	60.1	62.5	2.4
7	58.4	63.7	5.3
10	58.5	62.1	3.6
11	57.0	55.1	1.9
14	57.1	61.6	4.5
12	57.0	63.3	6.3
15	59.4	66.8	7.4
16	61.5	69.3	7.8
18	71.3	73.9	2.6
19	61.8	65.3	3.5

[2] Scores reported are the means for each college sample taking the Inventory of Beliefs developed by the American Council on Education Cooperative Study of Evaluation in General Education. As the circumstances under which the pre-test and post-test were administered were not always identical (including some differences in the elapsed time between the two at various institutions) those responsible for the study caution against precise comparisons among the institutions. The pre-tests were usually administered at college entrance and the post-tests toward the end of the freshman year.

A high score indicates a rejection of the authoritarian stereotypes of which the Inventory was composed, in other words a disposition towards "liberality" or flexibility of belief. Maximum score—120.

of the categorical way in which they are expressed rather than because of their intrinsic meaning. To the extent that the Inventory of Beliefs measures the degree of dogmatism in personality, the results of its use show that some change in student character, beyond the expressed opinions, may be under way in college. (15)

Students' capacity to think critically increases

Tests of "critical thinking in social science" show students acquiring greater capacity to reach judgments by reasoned thought instead of blind opinion or on the basis of someone's unchallenged authority. Again, the improvement is modest on an overall basis at most institutions, and is greatest with those who need it most. (1) One study does show specifically that those who have had a year's residence in college make a greater gain than those who have not. (112)

TABLE 16: Development of Critical Thinking in Social Science[3]

College	Pre-test	Post-test	Difference
1	33.1	36.9	3.8
6	25.6	29.4	3.8
7	21.9	24.8	2.9
8	22.9	30.7	7.8
12	24.1	33.8	9.7
14	23.1	24.9	1.8
15	22.7	28.9	6.2
17	23.8	26.6	2.8
18	32.1	36.8	4.7
19	24.0	28.2	4.2

[3] Scores reported are the means for each college sample on the Critical Thinking in Social Science test developed by the American Council on Education Cooperative Study in General Education. As the circumstances under which the tests were administered varied among institutions, those responsible for the study caution against precise institutional comparisons. A high score indicates a high capacity for critical thinking.

The college-educated are less prejudiced

Studies of prejudice show that more highly educated persons tend to have less prejudice toward racial and ethnic groups and to be more tolerant of political nonconformists. On racial attitudes, the difference in favor of college graduates as against those with less education is in the order of 10%-20%. (50, 51, 53, 58) Regarding civil rights for communists and radicals in general, the definitive study made for the Fund for the Republic establishes that a clear majority of those with a college education can be considered among the more tolerant third of the whole population, and only a very small percentage among the least tolerant fifth. This tendency persists in all groups and regardless of sectional, religious or other differences. (60) The Cornell survey and the Inventory of Beliefs confirm the view that students become progressively less prejudiced at college.

TABLE 17: The Tolerance of the Educated

(Data from *Communism, Conformity and Civil Liberties*, by Samuel A. Stouffer. Copyright 1955 by Samuel A. Stouffer; reprinted by permission of Doubleday & Company, Inc.) (60)[4]

Schooling	Less Tolerant	In-Between	More Tolerant
College graduate	5%	29%	66%
Some college	9	38	53
High school graduate	12	46	42
Some high school	17	54	29
Grade school only	22	62	16

(data from the Cornell survey)[5]

	Year in college				
	1	2	3	4	5
Anti-civil liberties	49	48	41	34	31
Pro-civil liberties	51	52	59	66	69

[4] Scores on the "tolerance scale" developed in this survey were used to differentiate the "more tolerant" segment of the population (31%), the "less tolerant" (19%) and the in-between group (50%). The findings are reported in terms of the percentage of each educational group whose scores placed them in one of these three segments.

[5] Percentage of students in each college year (including graduate school) who, on a scale of attitudes toward civil liberties, tended toward suppressing, or maintaining them.

But these conclusions are subject to several important reservations. The educational variable does not seem to govern all forms of prejudice with equal force. It influences some opinions more than others, especially those which hinge largely on the possession of knowledge or information. Where *emotional* attitudes are involved, the amount of a person's education plays a lesser part. For instance, the influence of education is less marked regarding attitudes towards the *social* rights of Negroes—willingness to eat in restaurants where Negroes are served, to reside with them or accept them in fraternities—than in regard to opinions concerning racial differences in intelligence, cultural contribution or moral character. (58)

Furthermore, the differentiating influence of education tends to work *with the grain* of the movement of social attitudes in the country at large, rather than against it. That is, if the point of view of their contemporaries shifts—towards lesser prejudice or towards greater—the attitudes of the college graduate shift also and in the same direction. There is thus no *fundamental* effect of education on prejudice but only a modest tempering of the prevailing mood. For instance, in the years from 1945-1953 Americans became much less tolerant of Communists. The shift in opinion among the college educated was just as marked as among the less educated, even though a somewhat larger proportion of the college group started—and remained—tolerant. Among the college educated, those who would deny freedom of speech to a Communist increased from 31% to 71%; among the less educated from 42% to 78%. The tide of national opinion thus swept the college educated along just as easily. Their tolerance was just as volatile. (55)

This same conclusion is implied in the data showing that the younger a person is, regardless of education, the more tolerant he is likely to be. The older college graduates tend to share the prejudice of their generation, rather than the tolerance of the "educated." For instance, among college graduates 60 and over, only 31% are included in the "more tolerant" category, whereas among those below 40, 75% or more are "more tolerant." This compares with 29% of high school graduates over 60 who are "more tolerant" and 44% under 40 who are so inclined. (60) Thus, as the whole pattern of American culture moved towards tolerance, during the last twenty-five years, the college experience made for even greater tolerance. The college student acquired—or perhaps anticipated—the outlook of his generation, only more so. But the fact of having had a college education, did *not* make the older generation either more disposed towards a tolerant outlook *per se*, or more flexible than others of their age in changing their original mind set to accord with the trend of the times.

There is further evidence to the effect that the influence of college in diminishing prejudice depends on operating within a favorable cultural context. Before the Second World War, studies of attitude changes in college frequently showed little or no change in regard to racial prejudice. (79, 150, 151) Since the War, however, increased racial tolerance is one of the most characteristic changes. During that period, of course, the United States had mounted a major ideological crusade against the doctrines of racial inequality and discrimination as propounded and practiced by the Nazis, and in the process had to reevaluate its own conceptions and conduct *vis à vis* its Negro, Jewish, and other minorities. The main "thrust" of the American disposition regarding racial differences shifted as segregation was abandoned in the Army, fair employment practices legislation increasingly ruled out economic discrimination, and even social and educational discrimination came under concerted attack as antidemocratic. College students quickly discovered if they had not before that prejudice was now considered unbecoming an "enlightened" American citizen. College thus became an effective medium of communication for a newly prescribed social value.

Students become more permissive in human relations

The college student is less prone than those with less education to categorize people as "weak" or "strong" and to adopt inflexible beliefs regarding human nature and capabilities. Here, as with racial prejudice, youth and education go hand in hand. The older generation and the less educated are the more likely to be "rigid categorizers." (60)

Greater flexibility is characteristic of college students' attitudes toward family relations and the bringing up of children. 15% to 25% more of the college graduates than of high school graduates (depending on their age) would allow children to talk back to their parents. (60)

Students seem to become less dogmatic and critical in judging human conduct as they progress through college, also more sensitive to human qualities such as tolerance, cooperativeness, and broadmindedness. Findings of a pre-war study at Ohio State using the Pressey Interest-Attitude Test anticipate those of the much more exhaustive inquiry at Vassar. Far fewer seniors than freshmen disapproved of such activities as "talking back," "playing hookey," "shooting craps," petting, divorce, or being an atheist. Seniors, more than freshmen, admired people who were tolerant, sympathetic, democratic, impartial, cooperative. (They also valued more highly such qualities as enthusiasm, resourcefulness, inventiveness and competence and having initiative. The senior proto-type was thus a strong human as well as a friendly one). (81)

The Myth of College Liberalism

When all is said and done, the value changes which seem to occur in college and set the college alumnus apart from others are not very great, at least for most students at most institutions. They certainly do not support the widely held assumption that a college education has an important, general, almost certain "liberalizing" effect.

This conclusion admittedly is at variance with the findings of a sizeable number of attitude studies, indicating a clear "trend toward liberalism with increasing exposure to academic influence." (106, 325) However, the following considerations warrant a revised estimate.

1) Most of the studies reporting significant change by students toward liberal beliefs in college were conducted in the 1930's when exceptional social and economic distress was prompting the most drastic reorientation of public philosophy experienced in American society. It would have been extraordinary indeed if this culture-wide social revolution had not penetrated the campus to some extent. But did the change of outlook on the campus move in front of the change in the country, or merely keep pace with it?

Unfortunately, none of these studies was in a position to compare the amount of change in the social and economic attitudes of college students with that occurring among youth not in college, or for that matter, among the population as a whole. Recent studies which do compare college graduates with others find the difference in outlook negligible on many questions. On economic issues the college man is likely to be more *conservative* than the others. (60, 61)

Looked at from another standpoint—in the perspective of time rather than of cultural context—a *long-run* shift in some values was under way, a "secular trend" to borrow the economist's concept. This ran parallel to many of the changes in student attitudes in the

30's and therefore accounts for at least part of the influence which has heretofore been attributed specifically to the college experience. For instance, a comparison of three undergraduate generations at Ohio State, in 1923, 1933, and 1943, showed that the modern student was freer from social and moral taboos, and had less anxiety connected therewith. (118) Also, a much larger proportion of the war generation approved of war, than did their depression predecessors. On the other hand, students changed little in their disapproval of divorce, strikes and socialism. Within each college generation the movement of attitudes followed the long-run trend, though the change from generation to generation was greater than from freshman to senior in the same generation. The persistence of these trends through depression and war lends weight to the conclusion suggested by the director of the study that the "general tone or climate of life" has changed, at least in regard to liberalizing the conventions of social conduct. If this be so, college students were merely keeping up with their times, rather than responding to a particular impetus from their educational environment.

2) Such liberalizing influence as college does exert beyond the secular trend, probably operates upon a superficial rather than a fundamental level, upon voiced attitudes toward broad, impersonal social policies rather than upon the decisive standards of personal conduct and human relationships.

The term "liberalism" (or "radicalism") as used in most of the studies does not refer to a well-defined, consistent pattern of values. It has been attached on a blanket and largely *a priori* basis to approval of social legislation, defense of the "freedoms," rejection of racial discrimination, and skepticism of a supernatural God holding a personal relationship to man. Do these various attitudes really hang together and distinguish a "liberal personality" or do they indicate only what some researcher (or his panel of consultants and "judges") personally conceives to be liberal?

Some of the very attitudes which might in the 1930's have marked a man as an independent thinker, and even a non-conformist, are today thoroughly conventional. What undoubtedly appears to many students' families as thoroughly unconventional thinking and behavior, is the sophistication, flexibility and social aplomb which will enable these students to get along easily with the kind of people who will be their own neighbors and associates after graduation. A liberal attitude, in the sense that a student will not let fixed moral standards or ingrained prejudices govern his relations with other people is almost an imperative "convention" of a society in which good business requires everyone to be treated with respect as a prospective customer.

Furthermore, some of the data cited above in regard to civil rights show how much and how quickly so-called liberal attitudes can shift with the current of popular opinion or public policy. Another example is the evaporation of "liberal" pacifism as the United States became progressively involved in the Second World War. If liberalism were a way of life, a fundamental organization of values that a student had acquired during college, one would expect greater steadiness.

The "liberalism" which was detected in these attitude studies, therefore, was not a liberalism of character, but only a random collection of opinions in vogue during a particular generation. The studies do not show that the student became a more liberal *person* in college, but only that he acquired, temporarily perhaps, some social and political attitudes that were representative of the outlook of his own time, rather than of his father's. As perceived by an admirably candid analyst qualifying the results of his own research, the attitude tests perhaps were measuring "verbalized liberality of attitudes rather than socially functioning personality." (81)

3) Still a further qualification must be entered concerning the significance of attitude changes during college. A selective process to a considerable extent foreordains that only students will come to college and succeed in staying through college who are already somewhat inclined toward the prevailing "college attitudes," or whose views are most susceptible to change in this direction. One study showed that high school students expecting to go to college tended to be less racially prejudiced and more devoted to civil rights than those who were not planning to go on to higher education. But politically and economically the college group was more conservative. (205) This corresponds exactly to the difference we have seen between college graduates and the rest of the population—the college man is to the right on politics and economics, and "liberal" on social and moral issues. Comparisons of students who drop out of college with those who stay on find the same contrast—the former

could not or at least did not sufficiently liberalize their attitudes at the proper points in order to fit in. (71, 286)

In conclusion, college has a socializing rather than a liberalizing impact on values. It softens an individual's extremist views and persuades him to reconsider aberrant values. It increases the tolerance potential of students towards differing beliefs, social groups and standards of conduct so that they can move about with minimum friction in a heterogeneous culture. It strengthens respect for the prevailing social order.

The Constancy of Basic Values

The changes which have been observed—moving students towards a greater uniformity and at the same time somewhat more flexibility of social outlook—are mainly changes on the surface of personality. They do not really involve the fundamental values which shape a student's life-pattern. The weight of evidence indicates that actually very little change occurs during college in the essential standards by which students govern their lives. The values with which they arrive and which are integral elements of their personality, are still there when most students leave. They may have modified their opinions on a lot of questions and have learned how to tolerate and to get along more easily with people of differing hues and views. They may have become more self-reliant. They may have changed vocational plans. But most students remain fundamentally the same persons, with the same *basic value-judgments*.

At Syracuse University, for instance, practically no difference in religious beliefs emerged as between freshmen and seniors. In regard to social values, seniors tended to avoid extreme positions more than the freshmen, but the differences were not profound. (41) Most of the surveys made of student "citizenship"—attitudes towards politics and political participation—show little if any change from freshman to senior year. At one college, renowned for its positive interest in encouraging students to undertake active political and civic responsibilities, seniors exhibited a more *negative* view than freshmen of politics and *less* interest in personal participation. (33)

The overall constancy of student values is convincingly demonstrated in several studies which compared freshmen and senior responses on the Allport-Vernon Study of Values. A number of these were able to test the same individuals when they entered college and again when they were about to graduate. With few exceptions, the differences between freshmen and seniors were so small as to be of little or no statistical significance. (71, 91, 102, 114)

An intensive study of the effect on individual students of transition from high school to college came to much the same conclusion for the period up to the sophomore year. (16) While some shifts in emphasis occurred, the individual's basic pattern of values remained unchanged. For the group as a whole, the religious and the political values somewhat declined, and the aesthetic and economic values rose slightly. The amount of change in certain values for some individuals was considerable. But close examination of each case revealed that the pattern was set *before* college, and that the direction of the change which occurred was consistent with the student's previous bent. Thus the values of the religiously inclined student became even more clearly and consistently pivoted around a religious hub; the student who started with a strong value for wealth became more devoted to this end during college, and subordinated or adjusted his other values accordingly. College—or maturity—contributed consistency, but did not effect a reorientation of values.

This is the broad conclusion, too, of the values survey conducted by the Cornell Social Science Research Center, both at Cornell itself and elsewhere. The upperclassmen by and large have achieved a synthesis of their values which reinforces their principal original motivations. College has firmed up their attitudes on most issues, and given them more definiteness. Fewer students straddle. But most of them have not changed the fundamental value-orientation with which they came to college. They have simply worked out a greater internal consistency within their value-system.

The College Impact on Religion

There is conflicting evidence on whether religious beliefs are susceptible to change during college or are among those basic values which remain largely immune from college influence. Some claim to detect a strong secularizing process at work leading toward the abandonment of religious conviction and practice. Others identify a trend away from orthodoxy toward "liberal" beliefs, but do not conclude therefrom that students necessarily become less religious. Then some recent surveys report a clear *upswing* in religious interest among college students. This was the impression of the University Christian Mission, conducted by the National Council of Churches. Finally, the implication of studies of values such as those noted above is that religion is an area where the fundamental pattern is set before college, to be changed if at all only in later life well after graduation.

Contemporary data do not indicate a major secularizing impact in college. The Cornell survey, limited though it was to non-sectarian institutions, noted a very widespread, and if anything, *rising* religious interest. (See Chapter 1)

TABLE 18: Changing Evaluation of Religion in College

In what way has your evaluation of religion changed,
if at all, since you came to college? (B-53)

	Value religion more	Value religion less	No change
UCLA	22%	17%	61%
Cornell	32	15	53
Dartmouth	36	18	46
Harvard	30	22	48
Michigan	32	20	48
North Carolina	34	12	54
Texas	33	14	53
Wayne	24	15	61
Wesleyan	49	16	35
Yale	36	19	45
Total (average)	32	16	52

For instance, for every student who stated that he personally valued religion less since he came to college, there were two who had come to value religion more. At none of ten institutions surveyed did the number of "defectors" equal the number of those whose value for religion had increased. Furthermore, fifty percent of the students felt they had *not* changed their initial evaluation. Similar inquiry of students at such religiously oriented institutions as Beloit and Springfield College brought an even higher response, 50% asserting their religious beliefs had strengthened during college. (71, 283)

Faithfulness of attendance at religious service may decline somewhat in college. (45) But so does it among youth of the same age who are not in college; and quite a large number of students at some institutions insist they go to church more often than before. (283) The early 20's appears to be the period in life when concern for religion is least. With parenthood, many persons stage a return to regular religious practice especially if they were reared to a devout faith. (45) There is no indication that a college education operates to break this cycle, though more adequate data, especially in the form of individual religious life-histories, are needed to confirm this impression.

A liberalizing of belief definitely occurs among *some* students in the course of their college education, and the influence in this direction is pronounced at *some* institutions. It was especially noted in attitudes studies made during the 30's which reported that seniors tended to believe less in a personal God and in prayer than did freshmen, were more critical of the church, and accepted fewer of the doctrines of supernatural determination of physical and human events. (71, 73, 79, 89, 106, 100, 109, 325) But the fact that the religious orthodoxy of students at many institutions remained almost totally unaffected would indicate that it is not college education *per se* which is responsible for any liberalization of religion that occurs. Perhaps influences peculiar to certain campuses, or the susceptibility of particular individuals bring about change in this direction. Paradoxically students who enter college with extremely rigid and fundamentalist beliefs appear particularly vulnerable to liberalization (106, 109), while institutions such as Clark, Springfield and Wesleyan, where the liberalizing influence is obvious, have a strong commitment to religious values (though not fundamentalist directed). (71, 79, 116)

The main impression, however, is that religious beliefs and the values related thereto, have been remarkably *persistent* through college, regardless of institution or the time when students were in college. One of the earliest intensive studies of student attitudes (109) found that at Syracuse the great majority maintained the concept of God and the attitude toward prayer they held as freshmen, though upperclassmen tended to believe somewhat more than freshmen in an impersonal God. There was little change in the expressed need for religion or interest in church. More than 20 years later after depression and World War II, another study of religious and social beliefs at the same institution came to almost identical conclusions. (41) Other surveys yielded similar findings at Northwestern, Wisconsin and Chicago. Different as their student bodies were in many respects, they maintained their respective views about God and church virtually unchanged throughout the college experience. (40, 76)

However, in later life, the individual's evaluation of religion may increase. A marked shift occurred among those whose outlook was expressed before the war on the Allport-Vernon Study of Values and who have recently been questioned again with the same instrument. (72, 80) This "return to religion" in the middle years is not necessarily to the orthodox religious beliefs of adolescence. The evidence is limited, but one series of penetrating interviews revealed views of God which were quite impersonal and rational—"liberal" in the sense in which the term has been applied in the attitude surveys. (82) College may well be too ephemeral an experience to mold so deep a part of life as a person's convictions of supreme reality, and his own relationship to it.

3

Influence of the Curriculum

To THE extent that students' values do change, or rather are modified, during college, how much is this the result of the content of their education? Does a liberal college education have a different effect than a professionally directed curriculum? Does an integrated program of general education leave a distinctive mark upon students' values? What outcomes can be traced to the students' work in social science, or to certain specific courses or types of courses?

Regrettably, the verdict of this report must be negative on almost all counts. We have found little evidence that the values of students change consistently as a result of the particular type of educational program in which they are enrolled or of the field of study in which they major. Objective evaluation of the outcomes of specific courses in social science under more or less controlled conditions indicates that they too rarely exert a distinctive impact on student attitudes.

Sometimes individual students subjectively attribute important influences to their courses. They say that their understanding of world affairs has increased, or even that they have chosen a different vocation as a result of certain of their studies. In a few cases a particular course has demonstrated a statistically significant (though relatively minor) effect on some value, for instance the diminishing of race prejudice. But most of the data yield no such result.

Some evidence suggests indirectly that comprehensive, well-organized, purposeful general education programs may have a stronger impact on student beliefs than curricula which are departmentally based and more conventional, but a generalization to this effect would be quite hazardous.

So little difference of outcome is associated with any phase of the curriculum, that one does not have to determine whether it is a selective factor—a typical predisposition of attitudes among students entering a given field of study—which accounts for a distinctive orientation of values at the end of their educational program. There is simply no major difference of values to account for.

The main bodies of relevant information are:

1) surveys which differentiate the opinions, interests and activities of students and alumni by the fields of study in which they have engaged;

2) analyses of changing beliefs at a spread of institutions which have differing types of curricula;

3) before-and-after tests of attitudinal and other changes in particular courses, or groups of courses;

4) student estimates of influential factors shaping certain of their attitudes, and their appraisals of the significance of certain courses.

What You Study Does Not Determine Your Values

The most conclusive evidence concerning the relationship of student values to the curriculum comes from the Cornell Values Survey. A breakdown of its results according to the field of study in which each student was concentrating or planning to concentrate, shows that the patterns of value are almost identical among students in the different fields—within each university and across the sample as a whole.

No significant differences distinguish the outlook of students interested in social science from the point of view of the rest of the students at their respective institutions on—human nature, family relations, political and economic philosophy, race, civic obligations including military service, religion or life-satisfactions. Even where the campus was heavily populated with prospective engineers, business administrators, natural scientists or agriculturists, the social science students ran with the pack. Only in regard to educational objectives was there a clear difference. The social science group tended to rank general education as more important than professional preparation.

Here are some of the issues where interest in and study of the social sciences could not dent the campus pattern of values:

Estimate of human nature: Social science students believe as much as others on their respective campuses that most people are inclined to look out for themselves rather than to help others; but also, that most people can be trusted. They are equally reluctant to categorize people arbitrarily into the "weak" and the "strong."

The well-ordered family: Social science interests make little difference in the attitude of students towards discipline in family relations. They split in just about the same proportions as their fellow students in other fields, on such questions as whether parents are strict enough today with their children.

(40% of the social science group as against 44% of the total sample believing they are *not* strict enough.)

Self-sufficiency and optimism: At most institutions in the survey students in social science were just about as confident as others (73% against 77%) that any man able and willing to work has a good chance of succeeding. The one clear exception was Wayne (in Detroit) where they were significantly less confident than students in other fields (only 44% as against 67% of the student body as a whole had such confidence). This may reflect a higher concentration in the social sciences of students from families which have experienced economic insecurity.

There was likewise very little difference of opinion on whether "It's who you know more than what you know that counts these days," (28% of the social science students agreed, 30% of all the students).

Confidence in the democratic process vs. political cynicism: Students in the social sciences are hardly more skeptical than others regarding the efficacy of the democratic process. They mirror their respective campuses almost exactly on such questions as:

	Percentage agreeing at 10 institutions among	
	Social Science	All Students
There's little use writing to public officials because often they aren't really interested in the problems of the average man	22	26
If people knew what was really going on in high places, it would blow the lid off things	31	37
The general public is not really qualified to vote on today's complex issues	52	47

Political candidates are usually run by
political machines   69   73

Philosophy of government: Despite their presumably greater interest
in and acquaintance with public affairs, students in the social science
field are just about as divided as their fellow-students in evaluating
the proper scope of governmental activity, though they are slightly
less dubious about the "welfare state."

	Percentage agreeing at 10 institutions among	
The best government is one which governs least	Social Science	All Students
The best government is one which governs least	28	33
Democracy depends fundamentally on the existence of free business enterprise	50	62
Government planning almost inevitably results in the loss of essential liberties and freedom	28	31
The "welfare state" tends to destroy individual initiative	52	60

Racial Tolerance: The social science group is no more—and no less—
tolerant of different racial groups than their fellow students, and they
are equally divided as to the desirability of legislating non-discrimination. The power of campus values to override any common perspective
which might stem from interest and study in social science is especially plain on these issues where the point of view is very different
at some institutions than others. At North Carolina, for instance,
44% of the whole student body agree that Negroes are lazy and
ignorant, and only 26% would approve of the Federal government
requiring employers to hire people without regard to race, religion,
color or nationality. The division of opinion of the social science
students is almost the same, 46% and 24%. Contrast Harvard, where
only 10% of the student body, and 10% of the social science group
believe Negroes to be lazy and ignorant, while 60% of the student
body, and 56% of the social science students approve of Federal fair
employment legislation.

Campus patterns of opinion also prevail among social science students on such questions as:

Outlawry of the Communist party (about 2 to 1 opposed)
Criticism of conscientious objectors
 (about 1 out of 3 would have them leave the country)
Charges of radicalism among faculty members
 (rejected by 3 out of 4, or more)

Attitude towards war: College by college, social science students are like their campus in regard to the proportion who consider war morally wrong (usually about 2 to 1), yet accept fighting for the ideal of free peoples against dictatorship (roughly 60-40) and acknowledge an obligation to protect one's government (about 2 to 1).

At Cornell and Wesleyan, social science students tend somewhat more than their fellows to rely on military power as a deterrent of war. But the difference is not great (58% vs. 41% at Cornell, 51% vs. 38% at Wesleyan), and at other institutions there is no significant difference. On the whole, social science has no observable effect on the extent of students' pacifism, skepticism, or nationalism, as they appriase the phenomenon of war, and the means of preventing it.

Religious belief and practice: Social science students are no less religiously-oriented than their campus as a whole, and they appear as little susceptible to "secularization" during college as other students, except perhaps at Wayne. At a couple of institutions (Michigan and Wayne) the social science group was not as regular in attending church, but the samples were small and the distinction is not necessarily constant. Certainly there is no evidence to support the view that interest and study in social science has a consistent tendency to reduce a student's sense of need of religion, or his devoutness.

Life satisfactions: A most surprising finding is that social science seems to make very little difference in a student's principal sources of satisfaction in life. Family and career are top choices for 90% of the students regardless of their field of study. 50%—60% include recreational activities among the three most satisfying. Generally there is no greater disposition among social science students than others on their campus to consider participation in public affairs at the community, national or international level an important source of personal satisfaction. Interest and study in social science apparently does *not* stimulate any unusual degree of social concern, or increase students' attraction to a civic role.

The only point at which students in the social sciences seem to differ even modestly from the patterns of campus values is in their evaluation of college objectives. At several institutions they tend more frequently than others to rank general education and appreciation of ideas as the most important educational ideal and fewer consider vocational training the primary aim. Also, a somewhat higher proportion of the social science group at some of the institutions consider the development of knowledge and interest in community and world problems *an* important goal of a college. The difference at most is one of relative emphasis, and it does not arise at all the institutions surveyed. More than likely, it represents the practical consequence of the social science group having a less precise vocational orientation to begin with than many of their fellow students. It surely does not indicate a fundamental difference of educational values or philosophy associated with a social science curriculum.

TABLE 19: Most Important Goal of the Ideal College

	Social Science	All Students
Provide vocational training; develop skills and techniques directly applicable to your career	15%	30%
Provide a basic general education and appreciation of ideas	48%	34%
Develop your knowledge and interest in community and world problems (% who considered this an important goal, but not the most important)	5%	3%
	60%	48%

DOES LIBERAL EDUCATION NOT LIBERALIZE?

It must be admitted that the findings just reported are at variance with conclusions reached in some previous studies, which indicated that students' values did differ considerably according to their fields of study and the type of curriculum they pursue. As a matter of fact the assumption is widely held that the more liberal the curriculum, the more liberal do students' values become and the better the quality of citizens who emerge from college.

The *Time* survey of college graduates made in 1947 determined that those who had majored in the social sciences and the humanities tended to be more civic-minded and to have a greater interest in political issues than the pre-professionally trained. (61) A survey of Syracuse alumni, using some of the same civic and political scales that Pace had previously constructed for the *Time* questionnaire, concluded that liberal arts students were inclined to have a higher awareness of public responsibility than the professional students and that this distinction carried over after graduation to a more active participation in community and political affairs. Their interest and attitudes were also better balanced and their political opinions more enlightened and better informed. (65, 191-193) In another Syracuse study some differences in the development of social values emerged among the various schools *after* the freshman year. Education and fine arts students developed significantly higher social concerns than those in applied science or business administration, although the interests and attitudes of freshmen were similar, regardless of the division in which they were studying. (41) These findings have led the Syracuse evaluators to conclude that "college does make a difference and the particular kind of college education also makes a difference." (112)

In direct opposition to the findings of the Cornell Values Survey, a number of studies in the 1930's noted a tendency toward political and economic liberalism among students majoring in the social sciences. Students in the natural sciences were less so inclined. (56, 73, 100) But at one college the reverse occurred—students of natural science proved most liberal and progressed most toward liberalism during college. (79) In another study, liberal arts students developed broader and more sensitive social values than students pursuing a commercial course. (38)

Differences also appeared in the response of students in various fields of study on the Allport-Vernon Study of Values. At Springfield College, social science majors showed a greater tendency to become socially concerned than physical education majors and less value for utilitarian and material satisfactions. (71)

In validating the revised Allport-Vernon values instrument after World War II, a number of important variations according to vocational interests appeared. Students of business administration held, as one might suppose, a much higher regard for economic values (what is useful and practical) than theological or medical students, and a markedly lower appreciation of social values (love of people and altruism). They also had the least "aesthetic" value (appreciation of form and harmony, and concern with the identities of experience). Engineering students were like the business administration group in most respects. Students of medicine held a higher theoretical value (interest in the discovery of truth) than the other groups; the ministerial students placed the least emphasis on this value, but naturally held far and above the highest religious value (appreciation of unity in the universe and eagerness to relate himself thereto, either by active affirmation of life or withdrawal from it). On the other hand, other occupational differences were not great. (310)

Few, if any, significant differences in the values held by students in various fields of study emerged however in such intensive analyses as the Study of the Transition from School to College (16) or Newcomb's study of changing values among Bennington students (85). Nor were fundamental differences among students in different curricula observed in a survey of religious and humanitarian attitudes at eighteen institutions. (39)

There are several factors which may account for the inconsistency in the results of these various inquiries. In many instances, a study was conducted at only one institution, usually the researcher's own, and there is no way of determining to what extent influences peculiar to that institution were at work to affect the response of the students. The fact that results were not consistent from place to place even when the same or similar instruments were used, suggests that such institutional factors may have been present. Certainly, the contradictory results would rule out any claim that a particular curriculum or field of study has a distinctive value impact which pervades the educational system.

Furthermore, the occupational differences in value emphasis which appeared on the Allport-Vernon revised Study of Values, were secured from relatively small samples of students in each category, and for the purposes of validating the instrument extreme contrasts were sought. No attempt was made to secure a broad representation of students throughout the country. So it is possible that many of these differences would shrink in a more general survey. Actually, the similarities of values among different groups of students were as noteworthy as the differences.

These studies have not been able to provide data about the students which would permit comparison of personality traits, previously held values, family background and other factors which might have helped to shape the values they held at the time they were surveyed. Thus *individual*, rather than field of study differences, might have accounted for some of the variations.

Finally, the degree of difference noted among the students in the various fields was usually quite small, so that though statistically significant, it was not necessarily indicative of a powerful and persistent influence upon values stemming from a particular type of educational program or area of study.

In any case, the data showing value differences associated with study of the social sciences (or liberal education in general) are so sparse, so contradictory, and on the whole so old that they can hardly offset the conclusiveness of the Cornell Survey. Unless some other factors are present, students are more than likely to be like their campus in the values they hold whether or not they choose social science as their field of study and regardless of whether they are pursuing a Bachelor of Arts, or a Bachelor of Science degree.

THE IMPACT OF PROGRAMS OF GENERAL EDUCATION

On beliefs

Some of the data from the American Council on Education Cooperative Study of General Education do imply that institutions with well-organized programs of *general* education may have a greater effect than others in liberalizing students' beliefs on a broad range of issues. Comparing the results of pre- and post-tests of the Inventory of Beliefs at two pairs of colleges, the Study noted:

Colleges A and B—both small liberal arts colleges with students' average scores high and nearly equal when the Inventory was first given— differed greatly in the amount of change over a one year period. Both schools have similar dormitory-living arrangements and a varied program of extracurricular activities. But at college A where change was greatest in belief, half of the freshman curriculum is a specially organized general education program. At B only one real general education course is taken in freshman year. Intragroup morale and informal out-of-class discussion of classroom experiences is greater at A.

Colleges C and D—two middle-western state-supported institutions with similar student bodies. Most of the students live in dormitories. Both have many courses in general education at the freshman-sophomore level. More students at D scored low on the Inventory of Beliefs, than at C; yet students at D gained more, and this was true regardless of the initial score. In other words the lowest scorers at D gained more than those with corresponding scores at C, and the same for those with high scores. The Study notes a main curricular difference in that general education at D is organized in a separate college, with courses required of all students, whereas at C general education is a division in the liberal arts college and is optional.

The two schools showing the greatest average gain in student responses on the Inventory of Beliefs had the following characteristics in common: 1) highly selected student bodies, 2) carefully integrated programs of general education, 3) classes conducted in small discussion sections with the teacher serving in the role of a moderator. (1)

Specific evaluations of some general education programs have shown positive outcomes. Courses at Drake University were held to have produced some of the behavioral changes sought (90), and freshmen at the University of Minnesota's General College gained in their socio-civic orientation and in knowledge of contemporary affairs (though many of their beliefs and prejudices did *not* change). (111, 123, 150) Freshmen at Michigan State developed more liberal beliefs by the end of their first year in the Basic College general education program (a gain of seven points on the Inventory of Beliefs was statistically significant and considerably beyond the .01 level of confidence). (138)

On critical thinking

The ACE Study found that students' capacity to "think critically" did not necessarily improve the most at those institutions which stressed critical thinking as an express objective of their general education curriculum or offered courses which deliberately sought to nurture this ability. On the other hand, the evaluators subjectively felt that some of the largest gains in critical thinking were made where the general education program as a whole was best organized during the freshman year. The college in the survey whose students gained the most put much emphasis on a comprehensive examination with thought-type items instead of questions calling for simple recall. (1) At San Francisco State, which also has an imaginative program for the first year, a third to a half of the students showed measurable improvement in objectivity, skill in reasoning, unified perception and breadth of awareness. Michigan State freshmen gained more than seven points on the ACE Test of Critical Thinking in their first year (statistically significant well beyond the .01 level of confidence). (138) Syracuse students gained 34% of the theoretical maximum they could gain on the ACE Test of Critical Thinking in Social Sciences, according to a special analysis of scores obtained in 1953.

A more general observation is that students of limited ability (as indicated on the ACE Psychological Test) tend to show the largest gains in critical thinking, particularly in social science courses. (1,138) Taken together, these findings may imply that those general education courses which service large numbers of students of average intellectual ability will realize a most important educational value if they succeed in stimulating critical thinking capacities, regardless of the amount of substantive ground left uncovered.

The prize example of the impact of a whole general education curriculum on student value-orientations appeared at Chicago during the Hutchins era. The extraordinary "intellectualism" of the student body (causing sensitive faculty some misgiving) was widely attributed to the Curriculum, devoted preeminently to the goal of "educating the mind." As seen in a penetrating appraisal made for the faculty of the College, Chicago students paid supreme homage to ideas. This was associated with a low spread of response to extra-curricular activities—social as well as "uplift" ones. The void formed by this absence of normal peer group activities was filled, but not completely—by endless discussion revolving around the issues raised in the curriculum. The unfilled part was left to loneliness. Hence the impact of the curriculum, in the judgment of this observer, was the most important influence on the lives of most Chicago students—but he did not consider it in all respects a healthy one. (285)

On value goals

Quite apart from the actual outcomes of special programs of general education, those institutions which have adopted such programs seem to have a keen interest in determining their impact on students—in terms of values as well as the acquisition of knowledge. They have either started evaluative studies or are eager to undertake them. Faculty and administration alike at these institutions are apparently committed to the proposition that education *should* make a difference in the values held by students and they want to know whether their programs do or don't. Whatever the impact on the students, the experimental programs in general education have apparently made educators more value-conscious.

THE SPECIFIC EFFECT OF SOCIAL SCIENCE COURSES

We turn now to a more pin-pointed examination of curricular influences. A review of over thirty attempts to detect and measure the effect of particular courses upon student attitudes, beliefs and sometimes conduct suggests (1) that significant change is the exception rather than the rule; but that, (2) some students have definitely changed opinions and perhaps values in the process of taking certain courses, (3) that the experimental design in most of these studies precludes a firm conclusion that it was the course that caused the change although a presumption that it did so is reasonable; (4) that the content and organization of these potent courses had little in common; but (5) most of them did deliberately set out to induce some sort of a value change among the students. One should not conclude from these experiments however that there are "packages" of social science materials which when presented as the content of a "core course" would have any more distinctive influence upon the body of students than other materials which might be selected.

Courses without value dividends

The following "before-and-after" studies which were undertaken to determine the value-outcomes of courses are among those which were unable to report extensive changes in the attitudes tested:

Antioch. (120) The ACE Inventory of Beliefs was completed by all freshmen at entrance and again near the end of the first term. Changes in belief were compared for four groups—those that had taken an introductory course in the History of Western Civilization, those that had taken the introductory course in American Government, those that had taken both and those that had enrolled in neither. The groups were relatively equal in respect to other academic factors, including the distribution of their remaining courses.

The conclusions showed that there was a highly significant change in beliefs (toward an increased rejection of "authoritarian" stereotypes) for *all* groups but that the change was almost the same regardless of the courses which the students had or had not taken. It made no difference (on the test as a whole) whether the students had had both of the introductory social science courses or neither.

Colgate. (75) A test of Critical Thinking in Social Science was given to freshmen at entrance in 1952 and repeated at the end of the sophomore year after a two-year general education program including a number of "core courses." No relationship was found between improvement in the test scores and the particular core courses which students had taken. In other words, whether or not a student had taken the social science core course in his program made no difference in his capacity to "think critically" in social science.

Harvard. (126) An extensive Value Profile (Bales) was administered at the beginning and near the end of an elective general education course in Human Relations. Preliminary analysis indicates that despite a very live and enthusiastic student response to the course, no appreciable change had occurred in the students' values even in those respects most immediately relevant to the content of the course.

Louisville. (149) Only slight, and for the most part, statistically insignificant changes in beliefs on social issues and attitudes toward social action resulted among freshmen taking a basic social science survey course.

Michigan State. (74) The most thorough study made of the impact of a general social science course has so far found a very limited student response of any kind, despite the strong emphasis placed by its staff on the encouragement of social values and the attributes of "democratic citizenship." Responses to the course (in terms of aspects of it which were liked or disliked) were classified into (a) those which were "achievement-oriented," e.g. concerned in one way or another with hurdling a college requirement, (b) "content-oriented," e.g. concerned with what was actually the substance of the course and (c) class or instructor-oriented. The bulk of the responses were of type (a); very few of type (c). The only factor so far discovered to have much association with the character of the student's response is his initially favorable or unfavorable attitude toward the course and its importance. Grades, the particular instructor teaching the student, student's urban or rural background, his economic status, etc. appear to have little if any connection with his responsiveness to the course. On the other hand, if he was favorably disposed to the course at the outset and thought it likely to be interesting or important, he tended to see more value in the content of the course per se rather than being preoccupied with "achievement" considerations. The implication is, what the student *thinks* a course may contribute is more influential in determining what he gets out of it than the content or instruction.

Another characteristic of the student response was the absence of fundamentalist tinged opinions regarding the merits of a "scientific" approach to social studies—this despite the strongly conventional religious background and pattern of beliefs of most M.S.U. students. This suggests the possibility of a hiatus between students' basic belief structure and their attitude toward the world of matter. In other words, it is no longer necessary to have consistency between one's religion and one's outlook on science, society, and education which is concerned with a science of society. "Science" and "religion" may now have become two separate, self-contained and self-justifying worlds, so that a student may comfortably tolerate at one and the same time a mechanistic approach to social relations and issues and a supernatural determinism on his personal religious faith.

Minnesota General College. (123, 150) A broad and varied evaluation of the outcomes of the General College program found that very few attitudinal changes had occurred among the students in the course of their two-year program of general education although it made a significant contribution to vocational preparation and a harmonious life adjustment. Students in the program were mostly of lesser scholastic aptitude than those who entered a full undergraduate curriculum.

New York University, Washington Square College. (135, 145) The effect of an integrated social science sequence of courses on students' political interest and attitudes was compared with the impact of a standard introductory course in American government and politics. No significant change took place in either, although the amount of time devoted to political affairs in the latter course was almost double that of the integrated course. Furthermore, no more significant influence resulted from a special section of the integrated course in which the instructor deliberately sought by selection of the course materials and personal emphasis and persuasion to promote a greater sense of political responsibility and interest in public affairs. Given the short run (three year) nature of the study, the type of student body and the possibility that latent rather than manifest changes may have been induced, the staff did not feel that as yet any far-reaching generalizations could be drawn from the data.

These results do not of course rule out the possibility of a "sleeper effect." Students' attitudes may change at a later date as the full import of what they have learned strikes home in facing concrete problems demanding action. (122) The short time span of most studies of this sort has precluded observing such a phenomenon—if it occurs. But on the basis of strong evidence that college attitudes generally persist with little change into later life, the odds run against the expectation that courses may have a significant delayed reaction. (83, 85)

A presumption that the content of courses will have only a very limited effect on students' values, either immediate or long-run, is also supported by a body of research on the relationship between attitudes and information. This has shown quite conclusively that the acquisition of factual knowledge rarely influences fundamental attitudes, especially those where the emotions are involved, for instance racial and ethnic prejudices. (50, 84, 115, 165, 201, 204, 301) Information seems to be a function of attitudes, rather than the other way around. Students pick out what they learn and retain, to fit what they already believe, rather than changing their attitudes to conform with a new body of knowledge.[1] (141)

Potent courses

Some social science courses do seem to have left a mark on many of the students taking them. At least students testify personally to an appreciation for the course and its meaningfulness to them. In a few cases, changes in attitudes or critical capacities have been objectively discerned. Students have tended to become more liberal on social and economic issues, to reject cultural stereotypes and surrender prejudices or to think more critically in reaching opinions and decisions after completing these courses.

These are exceptional responses, *not* typical, however. Furthermore, inadequate controls in some of the studies prevented their establishing whether the change was directly related to the course in question. This qualification is particularly pertinent to several studies conducted in the 1930's which purported to demonstrate that students acquired more liberal political and economic attitudes after taking sociology or other courses in social science. (125, 131, 325) The liberalizing

---

[1] A contrary conclusion is reached in a few studies. For instance, the Cornell Values Survey discovered that students' attitudes toward civil liberty correlated with their "intellectualism," and in particular with their college grades. Only 29% of those with grades over 85 were "anti-civil liberty" whereas 75% of those with grades under 69 were so disposed. See also the studies by Marcuse (110) and Smith (142). The weight of the evidence however is against "facts" having a substantial influence on values.

influence may simply have been "in the air," permeating the student generation or at least the particular campus. Or the course may have attracted an unusual proportion of students who were already disposed to be liberalized. These reservations, as a matter of fact, were spelled out by some of the investigators themselves. (140, 144)

In the following cases, however, the courses themselves seem to have had an unmistakable influence in changing attitudes and values:

Massachusetts Institute of Technology—Human Relations. This elective, upperclass course aimed to develop among prospective industrial executives a clearer understanding of the human factors involved in business enterprise and particularly a perceptive and sympathetic approach to the worker's position and outlook. Students' sensitivity in these respects did improve, as measured by their handling of a series of hypothetical situations in industrial relations. For instance, more students came to view human relations problems as resulting from the interaction of a variety of causes, rather than from the faults of specific persons or groups. They tended to develop a more positive attitude towards "workers" as a group. In general their understanding of human relations deepened. (130)

Michigan State University—Effective Living. This course, since abandoned, was a part of the general education sequence in the Basic College, required of all students during their first two years. It was a unique combination of subject matter, principally psychological and sociological, designed to improve students' understanding and critical judgment of human relations, and their capacities of social adjustment. A definite gain in "critical thinking" and a more friendly attitude toward minority groups developed, though these changes were not correlated with the students' acquisition of new knowledge in the field. Students who were least able to think critically to begin with gained the most in this regard. (165, 200)

New York University, School of Education—Introduction to the Social Studies. A sequence of courses, using a selection of social problems as the point of departure, was one option in the social science requirement for undergraduate teacher training. A general shift of social beliefs and values toward liberalism occurred, also an increased consistency of attitudes. Students made their greatest changes on issues of militarism and nationalism where they were least "liberal" to begin with. (124)

Pennsylvania State University—International Understanding. This course was recently introduced on an experimental basis primarily for students who were outside the liberal arts curriculum and had a very limited background in the social sciences. Its content departed radically from the usual courses in international relations and was deliberately designed, among other objectives "to so challenge the imagination and creative intelligence of the student that he acquires a genuinely critical commitment to those principles underlying a full, just and peaceful world."

Students after taking the course on its first run showed significantly less disposition to categorize people by national or cultural stereotypes than "control" groups of students who had not taken the course. This was demonstrated on several objective instruments which were given before and after the course. These results were emphatically confirmed when the course was repeated. In addition, it was the conclusion of the instructors that the course had had a widespread impact on students' basic approaches to international issues, including a marked lessening of chauvinism and a more critical attitude toward the use of power to preserve peace and security. A full report of the evaluation has not yet been made available, but the course is being continued and expanded, and there is every reason to conclude that this is a most promising curricular innovation. (137)

Syracuse University—Introduction to Citizenship. This distinctive offering of the Maxwell School of Citizenship has been required of students in the Liberal Arts College for many years as part of their general education, and a large number of students in the professional and vocational schools also take it as an elective. The course examines a series of vital issues of contemporary public policy. Although it sells no line and is at pains to present the main opposing approaches to the issues, it aims continually to get students to examine questions rationally, to arrive at personal judgments by critical thought and to arouse a sense of civic responsibility. A careful testing program over an extended period of time has demonstrated that students who take the course improve their critical thinking ability as applied to social issues more than those who do not, even though they start with the same capacity (as measured by ACE Critical Thinking in Social Science test, administered before and after the course, to matched groups). On the other hand, the course apparently has no appreciable effect upon *beliefs*. Students taking Citizenship 1 are not significantly different from others at the University. (112, 133, 146)

Intergroup education

A comprehensive analysis of college programs of "intergroup education" designed to reduce prejudice concluded that many of these efforts, curricular and other, did pay off. "Education, in the sense of planful efforts to change people," observed the directors of the College Study on Intergroup Relations ". . . can improve human relations. It can deepen intergroup understandings, liberalize attitudes, flow over into actions. We do not mean to imply that gains in any of these areas are large, or easy or certain. . . . But *educators can diminish prejudice.*" (53)

Some of the data on which this conclusion is based were summarized as follows:

Change Projects

	No. of projects	No change	Some change	Major change
Course content, school and college	83	22	37	24
Specific teaching methods	68	9	43	16
Campus activities	64	5	23	36

(The results were sometimes determined by pretesting and endtests; in other instances by the observations of participants in the projects or reports by those conducting them.)

Experimental Attempts to Reduce Prejudice
(from Arnold Rose, *Reduction of Prejudice*)

	No. of projects	No change	Change	In-definite
School or college course	13	4	8	1
Films radio	14	9	4	1
Personalized contacts	9	3	3	3
Correlation studies, knowledge with attitudes	12	9	2	1
Years spent at school or college	18	8	6	1

On the other hand, a close look at some of the projects evaluated in the above summaries, especially those at the college level, shows that relatively few were able objectively to measure their outcomes. 12 out of the 18 college projects which used before-and-after tests of attitudes demonstrated some degree of reduction in prejudice. These included sociology classes at New York State Teachers College, Albany (in one of which students participated directly in a project aimed to change community prejudices), a social studies course at Marshall College, Huntington, West Virginia, and a course in child development at the University of Florida, using "group-work processes" of teaching. But at several other teacher training institutions—

in Michigan, Minnesota, Wisconsin and elsewhere—changes were not impressive.

International education

The Carnegie Endowment survey of the Universities and World Affairs found at quite a number of institutions that academic training in international relations had some positive effects upon student understanding of world affairs. Students at a selection of southern colleges who had had more courses and specialized training in the international field consistently surpassed random samples of their fellow-students on a knowledge test. (21) This also happened at the University of Iowa where a careful analysis showed students with social science background to be better informed on world affairs. (163) But whether this superior grasp of facts vitally affected the students' opinions and *judgments* on issues of international policy is not apparent.

These experiences are the only ones so far uncovered where the *content* of the course seems clearly to have had some general "measured" influence upon student patterns of value or their methods of reaching value judgments. Even these have not registered changes of such magnitude as to justify the conclusion that they are models which could be offered anywhere by anyone with similar results. Nevertheless, there is a distinctive *purposefulness* about each one which motivated its organization in the first place and has guided its planning and conduct since. Each in its way was an experiment designed to make some specific difference in the students' outlook or attributes, without however propagating a set of doctrines. Perhaps it was the unified, coherent and well-defined philosophy of the course, and the resulting clarity of the values it presumed to encourage which made for its unique effectiveness.

STUDENT EVALUATIONS

If one considers what students themselves say their courses have meant to them, the curricular influence appears more significant than the record of measured changes of attitudes would indicate. Students have been generous in crediting their courses or college education as a whole with promoting their intellectual growth—changing their vocational interests and choices—and giving them "a burning desire for further self-education"—encouraging their civic participation—

making them more religious—broadening their understanding of others—making them more concerned about social justice—increasing their understanding of world affairs—opening up value questions—changing their ideas and actions—and just generally "stimulating" and "exciting" them. (See Inventory of Data, Section III B for listing of some student evaluations of course influences).

Not all student and alumni comment is so complimentary. On the whole, programs of general education fare rather badly in student opinion, and the felt outcomes of general social science courses in terms of influencing values and attitudes have been particularly discouraging. Two-thirds at one college could recall nothing in their educational experience that had stimulated political interest or concern for public affairs. At another institution, no general education courses in social science were marked as valuable by a majority of the students surveyed. At a third, more than an average number of students wrote off as a waste of time a pioneer integrated course in social science which to outsiders seemed to have an unusually challenging approach, fresh and well-presented content and a clear sense of direction. Students who are already set on professional or business careers are especially critical of general education courses as "not practical" and some even become bitter if required to take such courses. (167)

Actually, most student evaluations cannot qualify as discerning evidence of basic educational outcomes, considering the manner in which they have been made. Students usually indicate whether or not they consider that a course (or the college curriculum as a whole) has had some given influence upon them (with a checklist of items presented to ease the chore of answering). Rarely does the procedure require the student to weigh the *relative* influence of his courses in comparison with other factors. Furthermore, students are in reality solicited only for their off-the-cuff *impressions* rather than a reflective and discriminating self-inquiry which might reveal to themselves as well as to others just where and in what concrete ways a particular course had entered their lives and influenced their beliefs or conduct.

One of the critical gaps in educational research is a body of carefully collected autobiographies from students and graduates which provide a more personal insight into the influence of the educational process.

4

Impact of the Instructor

An accumulating body of evidence indicates that the person of the instructor is on the way out as an educational factor at many institutions. The teacher appears to have little standing with the mass of students, and less influence. He goes with the books, the blackboard, and "audio-visual aids." So limited is his personal impact, either within or outside the classroom, that one wonders whether the American college and university is coming to function not as a community of scholars but a cafeteria of learning where at appointed mealtime, standardized portions of intellectual victuals will be dished out by professional servers.

The large size and impersonality of today's universities undoubtedly contribute to a depreciation of the role of the instructor. But this cannot fully account for the phenomenon, as the instructor fares little better at many small residential colleges. Nor does quality of instruction appear to be the decisive factor in determining the impact of a teaching staff as a whole on the students. Though the dynamics and skill of an exceptional teacher undoubtedly increases his individual impact, one can often find instruction of high quality (by a teacher's yardstick) at places where overall impact remains low.

Fortunately, the phenomenon of robot instruction has not yet become universal. There are still colleges where the teacher counts with his students. High instructoral impact is more likely to be found at places where (a) contact between faculty and students in the curriculum is intimate, (b) the faculty is "student-centered," and teachers derive a real sense of satisfaction and value from teaching their particular students (regardless of their intellectual level, social background or outlook), (c) faculty (and perhaps students) have a relatively large amount of responsibility for the educational program of

78

the institution, (d) the institution, including its administration, is self-conscious and purposeful about its educational mission, and (e) there is wide diversity in the background, personality and values of the students.

THE LOW ESTEEM OF STUDENTS FOR THE INSTRUCTOR

The principal index now available of a teacher's influence upon his students, especially in regard to personal attitudes and values, is their own estimate of him. Student ratings of faculty have become established practice at a growing number of colleges, and when properly designed have proven quite reliable in determining the student's considered judgment of his instructor's various contributions and limitations. Students take the responsibility seriously and generally give candid opinions. The rating process does not turn into a popularity contest, nor is there a consistent tendency to favor the "authorities" of high rank as against younger and less renowned faculty. A student's grade in a course does not seem to influence his estimate. (217, 219, 221, 225) Furthermore, investigation has shown that the ratings are not ephemeral, but coincide very largely with the judgments given by students years after they have graduated. (213)

On the other hand, these data go only part of the way toward providing insight into the influence of the teacher. They tend to show mainly how much a student *likes* and *approves* his teacher, rather than what difference the teacher has made, if any, in his personal attitudes and value judgments. The latter is probably too subtle and prolonged a reaction for a student to appraise clearly, especially when he has hardly completed a course. Once more, we feel the lack of educational life-histories giving the sober reflection of a broad sample of graduates as to who and what exerted real influence on them in college.

Nevertheless, there is undoubtedly some relationship between the factors which cause a student to like an instructor and the kind of influence which the instructor can exert. An instructor who is unable to capture his students' approval and secure a generally favorable response from them would hardly have a profound impact upon their values (unless he so antagonized them that they developed some fresh hates and prejudices). (218) Analysis of the *criteria* which students use to identify the "good" instructor and the "poor" one will therefore indicate indirectly what it is that they look for in the teacher and hence what probably screens his contribution to them.

The good teacher: A composite of the traits which in student eyes mark the succesful instructor are:

1) Ability to arouse interest and enthusiasm. Depending upon the students, this may imply either skillful showmanship or intellectual excitement and provocativeness. A sense of humor helps. In the social sciences, a special premium is placed on the man who can stimulate "ideas."

2) Interest in students, cooperativeness and sociability, or more positively put, "empathy" for students. This quality is not considered as important at some institutions (Purdue, Brooklyn) as at others (University of Washington, Oklahoma A. & M.).

3) Tolerance and respect for students and their ideas, and giving those that want it an opportunity to get into the act in the teaching process; sympathetic consideration of their objections and complaints.

4) Clarity in the presentation of the subject matter, an ability to explain and to "structure" the material so that students can easily follow, understand and remember.

The poor teacher: Conversely, students dislike teachers who do not plan their courses well, do not explain clearly what is expected on examinations, oversimplify or overcomplicate or are just plain dull. But the blackest trait a teacher can have is disrespect for the students. He incurs acute disapproval if he talks down to them or otherwise belittles them. Sarcasm is an unpardonable offense. (210, 212, 216, 217, 220, 223, 225)

If these are the qualities which make or unmake a teacher with his students, what is likely to be the character of his influence upon them? Is not his primary function to make them comfortable as they go through the learning side of college, and for those who are "brains" to titillate their minds? Without disparaging the worth of these preferred instructoral traits, they tend by themselves to cast the ideal teacher in the role of a psychiatric baby-sitter. His contribution to the values of his students can hardly extend to a broadening of the horizons of their social obligations, to sensitizing their feelings towards others, or deepening their perception of moral truths. There is hardly allowance even for the breeding of real independence of mind, fundamental respect for intellectual integrity and devotion to the pursuit of knowledge. These are not what the student expects of his teacher, or values him for. Instead, he looks to his teacher to increase his self-assurance, self-respect, self-enjoyment and possibly his self-knowledge. He wants gentle nurture for his ego, while he gingerly tries out his intellectual wings. Especially, he wants someone to interest him and to give him directions (which he can passively copy in his notebook) to that "rich, full life" which he craves. The student appreciates the teacher who can give so exciting a performance that he is absorbed vicariously in the drama of learning without ever leaving his box seat.

The student ratings imply, therefore, that the *entire function* of the teaching profession has fallen into low esteem, not that students are unusually critical of their particular teachers. Indeed, students by and large commend their teachers. 75% or more of the faculty at most institutions get at least a "good" rating or its equivalent. The teachers in other words pass as "good fellows." But they do not carry weight. They do not cut deep. They do not disturb, shock—or quietly touch—the well-springs of motivation.

More explicit information demonstrates the lack of faculty impact on students at certain institutions.

Michigan State. (74) Analysis of student opinion concerning the basic social science course (obtained through intensive interviews with a random sample of those enrolled in 1953) showed that few students were "instructor-oriented." That is, they expressed relatively few judgments concerning the teacher's role in the course, as compared with comments on the assignments, the examinations, lighting, heating, the behavior of their fellow students and their own participation in class. Such comments as were made tended to be critical, but on the whole students were simply indifferent to the teacher. Further, there was no significant difference in the tone or character of the students' responses which could be associated with their having studied under a particular instructor (although over 20 different instructors of widely varied personality, outlook and background taught the course).

The instructors appeared, to an outsider, to be able and dedicated teachers, enthusiastic about their subject, eager to get student participation in class, and sensitive to the need of relating the course to student interest and experience. They were obviously distressed at the lack of student responsiveness, and their inability to shake the atmosphere of dullness which pervaded the classes.[1]

[1] An examination of student opinion concerning another basic course at Michigan State also reported a generally low rating of instructors. (165)

San Francisco State. (173, 223) Despite high student opinion of the faculty's personal qualities, lectures, class discussion and knowledge of their subject, students did not appear so favorable in regard to the faculty's success in "motivating" students. Furthermore, 40% indicated they had never spoken with their instructor outside of class. 25% said that they did not think their instructor was interested in their personal and social adjustment.

Further negative evidence concerning the influence of faculty on students is the fact that applicants for the Woodrow Wilson Fellowships, who are among the cream of the country's graduating classes in the humanities and the social sciences, rarely refer to their teachers when presenting a detailed account of the development of their intellectual interests. (186)

Obviously, the illustrations just cited do not sum up the situation for all of American higher education. They are at most straws in the wind, suggesting that we should not take for granted today the beloved assumption of educators that a noble and lasting influence results from the personal and subtle communion between teacher and student. Perhaps a new, more impersonal relationship is taking over on the campus.

The fault is surely not entirely the students', unresponsive though many of them undoubtedly are to the best of the best teachers. Student leaders point out that the faculty for their part often rebuff student initiative looking toward a more personal relationship. Frequently they complain that the teacher so insists on the primacy of the classroom and is so indifferent to out-of-class interests and activities that he has no real common meeting ground with students. A genuine student desire for close faculty-student relations—a "partnership in education"—frightens many faculty as they contemplate what this involves in terms of time, surrender of personal privacy and, even more, entering the unfamiliar world of student life where they do not enjoy the security of professional competence. (215)

WHERE FACULTY COUNT

It would be unfair and unreal, however, not to recognize the validity of the individual testimony of many students and alumni to the influence of one or more of their teachers upon their personal interests, approach to human relationships, and even the basic direction of their lives. This kind of evidence is hard to gather in any systematic way and harder yet to evaluate because it is so personal, subjective and variable.

Yet it is surely significant that when students are asked what factors aroused an interest in world affairs, many of them promptly credit their faculty. Whether the faculty have as much influence in this regard as other factors such as the press and radio, contacts with foreign students or even lectures and convocations is open to question. A survey by World University Service found fewer students noting faculty influence than these other factors but this study suffered from some ambiguities which limited its significance as a gauge of relative influence. (28) On the other hand, the Carnegie Endowment survey of the Universities and World Affairs found faculty and courses consistently mentioned most frequently as stimulants of international interest. (26)

It is clear that some teachers have much more influence than others. Columbia College alumni repeatedly and spontaneously mentioned one person as they considered what had been most important in preparing them for civic leadership and giving them a sense of social responsibility. Half a dozen other names were tossed in the hat—and then a large number just said "faculty." (174) An experiment at New York University School of Education showed that a particular instructor in an introductory social science course had more influence in liberalizing the attitudes of his students than others teaching the same course and by identical methods. (124) So with the stimulation of critical thinking. One institution broke down the gains made by students in different sections of the same course on the ACE Critical Thinking in Social Science test and concluded that who the instructor was did have a significant effect. (165)

Student responsiveness to the faculty is much greater at some institutions than others. The quality and nature of the faculty and of the student body at such colleges is not distinctive, at least by objective standards, as compared with places where faculty influence appears much more restricted. It may be that the character or climate of the whole institution has something to do with increasing the potency of its faculty. This institutional quality will be considered more specifically later, but some examples are appropriate at this point of colleges where an unusual faculty impact seems to obtain.

The World University Service survey of world-mindedness on thirty campuses, despite its methodological shortcomings, did plainly show that more students at certain colleges than at others appeared conscious of their faculty as a factor in their thinking about international affairs. Among the "high faculty influence" colleges were Lewis and Clark (Oregon), Macalester (Minnesota), Miami (Ohio), Park (Missouri), College of the Pacific (California), Pembroke (Rhode Island). There are some significant similarities among these institutions: their limited size, their well-defined educational objectives (three are Presbyterian-affiliated, considered among the most progressive and educationally dynamic of this group of denominational colleges), their internal cohesiveness. (28)

At Sarah Lawrence College, a tremendous personal influence of faculty with students seems to prevail, both in regard to academic matters and life planning. Each girl has an unhurried, intimate weekly conference with her "don" who is usually one of three instructors with whom she does all her work in any one year. She also meets frequently with her other professors out of class. If good rapport is not established between a student and the "don," a reassignment is worked out. In the end the student has had a very close and usually a congenial relationship with 8 to 10 faculty during her college career, and has thrashed through with them the whole gamut of value-issues which concern her. The profound influence of these individual teachers and advisors appears in self-appraisals made by students of their personal and educational development, as well as in college records. (88)

Macalester College is another institution where student respect for the faculty is high and acknowledgment of their influence widespread. Certain individual instructors were singled out by students and faculty alike as having exerted a significant impact on attitudes, choice of majors, vocational choices, extra-curricular interests, etc. It seems more than coincidence that the two Woodrow Wilson Fellows from Macalester selected in 1955 were among the few who referred explicitly in their application statements to the influence of particular faculty. On the World University Service survey (which at Macalester covered over 90% of the student body) faculty influence in regard to international affairs was noted by a high proportion of students in comparison to many of the other institutions surveyed.

THE TEACHER'S ROLE IN PROGRAMS OF GENERAL EDUCATION

A question of special concern to the present study is whether the role of the instructor is enhanced, or further undermined, when he teaches in the basic integrated courses characteristic of many programs of general education. The evidence so far available does not provide a clear answer.

On the one hand, many of the faculty associated with such programs feel that the impact of the instructor has been strengthened as a result of this type of general education curriculum. They are personally enthusiastic about their teaching, have a sense of common purpose in the program, participate in the gigantic task of curriculum revision which is usually involved in getting a general education program under way, and customarily place a high value on the teaching task in contrast to research and other educational functions.

On the other hand, observation of some general education programs, especially in social science, arouses some misgiving. There is a tendency for the integrated type of course to become standardized, especially when it is a widely required course. Once it is standardized, the program necessarily limits the individual discretion of the instructor to choose materials and to direct his teaching in a way which he finds most congenial and contributive to creative rapport with his students. The law of economy of effort works to limit the amount of year-to-year revision which is undertaken, thus depriving new staff of the opportunity to participate in the process of planning which proved so intellectually stimulating to those who organized the course in the first place. Then as the rut is worn deeper, both old and new staff lose some of their sense of personal excitement in the teaching experience and hence some of their capacity to spark student excitement in the learning experience.

The question then is, does the integrated type of general education program tend to rob the instructor of the degree of intellectual challenge necessary to keep *him* challenging to his students? Or put another way, does such a curriculum tend to make the instructor so much a *teacher* that he ceases to be a learner, and hence loses a fundamental tie with his students?[2]

In addition, special career problems beset the teacher in an inte-

[2] This assumes that a relationship of mutuality between teacher and student contributes to the value-outcome of education. Unfortunately, some studies indicate that an authoritarian relationship between teacher and student may be more conducive to learning and psychologically more congenial for many students. This could imply that general education, taught didactically would *increase* the impact of the instructor on students of "dependent" personality. (See Chapter VII)

grated general education program. He usually has no departmental status in one of the traditional disciplines, and he is not climbing the customary academic ladder of published research in a specialized subject. When he looks for an improvement of his position, or wants to transfer to another institution he has no standard "coin of the realm" to offer to departmental chairmen either in terms of the courses he has taught or his scholarship. This uncertainty about his professional future gnaws away at the morale of many an able younger instructor of a general course, and is undoubtedly one of the factors chiefly responsible for the heavy turnover rate in the staffs of these courses. (233)

Several institutions have attempted to meet the problems of the instructor in general education. Some feel they have done so successfully. Columbia College claims that twenty-five years of examination and re-examination of the results of the sequence in Contemporary Civilization have brought the course to a high degree of standardization *without prejudice to the initiative of individual instructors*. Its formula is to draw the instructors from four cooperating regular departments so that every man has his own departmental home. Rarely does one man teach more than one section and he is consciously encouraged to teach it in terms of his own interests, training and predilections, though using the common syllabus. (198)

The approach at Michigan State is different. A completely separate division administers the general education program and each of the basic courses is the responsibility of a special department with its own budget. Instructors devote their full time to the one course, are given pay and rank equivalent to men of similar tenure and experience in the standard departments (which offer courses only at the upperclass or graduate level). They are encouraged to pursue individual research interests and supported generously in this regard. The general education departments try to develop permanent staffs and invite instructors to come on the assumption that they will make their career in this kind of teaching. (202)

A similar approach is taken at M.I.T. in regard to staffing their basic course in the Humanities.

University of Minnesota has attempted a combination of the two approaches. A Department of General Education with a separate budget conducts the integrated basic courses (which are offered on an elective basis however rather than being required of everyone). Special staff is hired to teach but in addition a number of men from other departments teach sections and sometimes even head particular courses.

San Francisco State has experimented with a variety of special methods to build staff morale and give cohesion to its general education instruction without undercutting individual initiative. It takes pains to orient new staff members, encourages friends to visit each other's classes on an informal basis, and has promoted the concept of "cooperative staff groups" in which all the teaching personnel for a given course join in its design, evaluation and revision. An annual faculty conference brings the entire teaching staff together for a thoughtful review of a major educational problem of the college. (237)

None of these institutions has licked the problem of turnover however (except possibly Columbia). And the teacher's dilemma of keeping up adequate personal initiative in a standardized course is always present.

5

Effects of Teaching Methods

Educators have long sought the secret of how to teach most effectively and the body of research undertaken to this end is staggering. Much of this work has focused on the question of transmitting learning-how to help students secure the best possible grasp of a body of knowledge. But recently, studies have turned to the issue of whether particular methods of teaching can more markedly affect students' attitudes, values and even personalities.

Meticulously designed experiments have tested the non-intellectual as well as the academic outcomes of "permissive" as against "directive" techniques, "student-centered" or "therapeutic" as compared with "instructor-centered" or "subject-centered" teaching, and instruction by discussion vs. lecture, or recitation-drill. The trial of TV as an educational medium has opened an entirely new front in the battle over methods. In another direction, the introduction of "laboratory practices" or the adoption of the "case-method" or "problems approach" in social science courses has been urged against the traditional textbook approach as more effective in stirring students' interest in the social and political problems of the contemporary world and arousing concern to do something about them. Controversy over the implications of these experiments still continues partly because some of the results have seemed contradictory or too scattered and impressionistic to be conclusive, partly because devotees of one approach or another are so completely convinced of its peculiar merits. The present synopsis sheds no new light on the issues but tries only to determine whether the evidence as it stands justifies a broad conclusion that *how* students are taught may make an important difference in the values they hold and the decisions they reach on what they do.

The conclusion is that, on the whole, attitudes and value judgments are relatively unaffected by the manner in which students are taught. Some students may respond better to one method than another, depending on their particular personality and psychological needs. But no consistent outcomes have yet emerged from the use of a given technique. This verdict does not necessarily apply to those approaches which have modified the content of the courses so as to involve students in active value-laden experiences where they personally confront and decide controversial issues. Experimental evaluation of the outcomes of such practices has not yet really gone far enough, but one can draw a reasonable inference that this kind of instruction does carry greater impact than a straight "book course."

Student-Centered Teaching

During the last dozen years, a considerable effort has been made to apply to teaching, principles developed in psychotherapeutic counselling and guidance (especially as expounded by Carl Rogers and his disciples), and also the findings of group dynamics psychology. This has taken various forms, but the essential aim has been to get students to take a very personal and active part in the conduct of the teaching operation, even to the point where they, rather than the instructor, decide on the topics to be considered, the tempo of the course, and how their achievement is to be evaluated—by examination or otherwise. Discussion is obviously a *sine qua non* of the procedure, but a further qualification is that the instructor must avoid directing the discussion too much, and refrain from "giving the right answers." The teacher's job is to encourage each student to unravel a problem by his own thought process, or in conjunction with his fellow students. The exponents of this approach have urged that it would result in much more lasting and meaningful learning, and might also significantly affect students' values without sacrificing too much of the "substance" of a subject as taught by more conventional methods.

A series of controlled experiments at different types of institutions has pitted student-centered teaching against other methods under conditions where other educational influences, including the instructor's personal influence, were held relatively constant. (See Inventory of Data for reference to the principle studies.) One limitation has been the fact that most of the studies have been conducted with "captive audiences"—students in classes under the supervision of the investigators—and this has meant that most of the teaching has been in psychology. Whether different results would come about if the methods were applied to other subjects is not certain.

The experiments did not all yield identical results. However, after discounting an element of wishful interpretation on the part of some of the investigators, the following generalizations seem tenable:

1) There is little to choose, so far as student achievement in learning the substance of the subject is concerned. Students taught "permissively" usually do about as well as others (sometimes a little better actually) on objective tests of knowledge acquired by the end of a course. (124, 242, 246, 247, 249, 252)

2) Likewise, the method used makes no major difference in changing students' attitudes and beliefs. (124, 246, 247) In a few cases, student-centered teaching appeared to have accomplished a greater reduction of prejudices. (243, 251) But this result did not appear in experiments at other institutions. (241)

3) Students tend to be more dissatisfied with a permissively taught course and experience a sense of frustration and lack of achievement (though the latter is usually unwarranted as indicated in 1) above). The experience is of course radically different from their previous education, and they are often worried about keeping up their grades in this uncharted sea. (243, 244, 249, 252, 257; but contrast 241)

4) Some of the studies do make out a case for student personality growth, improvement in emotional and social adjustment and self-insight as a result of the novel method of teaching. (241, 242, 244, 245, 250)

5) One study indicates that a group-directed approach in teaching may result in group decisions or "norms" having a greater influence on the opinions of individual students than either the instructor's or their own considered judgments. (248)

6) The personality of a student and his orientation when he first comes to class has a lot to do with his reaction to the method of teaching, and what he gets out of the course. Individual differences among students are more important than differences of instructional technique in determining the educational impact. (246, 249) A student's feeling of freedom is an important variable, concludes McKeachie in an able summary of the present state of research on this problem. A class where the instructor insists on being "non-

directive" may increase the student's feeling of helplessness. The success of such teaching may well depend on the presence of individuals in the class who have had previous democratic group experience and have a positive attitude towards it. (249)

The findings of two recent experiments illustrate the present trend of research concerning the effects of student-centered teaching. Allport and Wispe examined various results of teaching sections of a course in Social Relations at Harvard by "directive" and "permissive" techniques. (252) Johnson and Smith at Michigan State studied the achievement and attitudes of psychology students under "democratic leadership." (246)

(a) The principal conclusion of the Harvard study was that teaching effectiveness was dependent not so much on the method used, as upon its relationship to patterns of student needs. "Intro-punitive students who had high needs for structure," were caustic about sections and instructors when placed in a "permissive" classroom situation. Students with "high autonomy needs, who were extra-punitive," were extremely critical when put into a directive classroom. Students who were "satisfied" had relatively favorable attitudes towards the sections and the instructors. Wispe concludes that "in order to maximize the learning process, teaching procedures must be made to articulate with students' needs. . . . students have learned different ways of reducing classroom tensions, and the best teaching method for some students is not the best teaching method for all students."

Among the more striking specific findings in the Harvard study were: directive teaching was preferred by a majority of the students; 51% wanted more direction (regardless of the kind of teaching they were receiving) as against 23% who wanted more permissiveness; the grades of the "bright boys" were not influenced by the kind of teaching received, but the dull boys profited more from directive-type teaching. Wispe suggests that permissive teaching might not have had an adequate trial, its full values perhaps not being realized in a class meeting once a week for one semester. This reservation is much to the point, since American students generally enter college so accustomed to directive instruction, including the paraphernalia of examinations, that they cannot be expected quickly to adapt to an entirely different frame of reference.

(b) In the Michigan State study, neither students' academic

achievement nor their attitudes toward democratic social processes were consistently affected by the kind of instruction they received (straight lecturing vs. largely permissive discussion with the class making many group decisions). There were interesting individual differences, however, in the response of students within the democratically taught sections:

Students under "democratic" instruction who most willingly accepted group decisions made *lower* gains in academic achievement.

Students who had a previous record of high grades became more favorable towards democratic teaching procedures. Being more secure academically they apparently felt more inclined to try something new.

Those most fully accepted by the other members of the class, liked it the best.

But the isolated individualist made the greatest academic improvement.

The inquiry's overall conclusion is that the most effective class is one where a) content is organized to facilitate team activities, b) a warm objective relationship prevails between instructor and student, c) a considerable amount of authority is delegated to the students, d) the grading system is designed to encourage incentives to group activity, participation and responsibility. But the decisive factor in a student's response will be the orientation which he brings to class and the favorable or unfavorable attitudes he develops in the first few days of class.

THE SIGNIFICANCE OF DISCUSSION

Quite apart from the particular psychological twist given to discussion as it is used in the student-centered approach to teaching, discussion *per se* has long been advocated as distinctly superior to lecture or recitation and drill as a means of making education more meaningful and personal to students. It has the special merits, according to its defenders, of eliciting a total response from the student personality, encouraging responsible evaluation and bringing the student to an appreciation of synoptic perspectives. In the judgment of a skilled practitioner of the art, "sustained discussion with an imaginative teacher and a powerful reading program has an openness that the lecture cannot have as an avenue of discovery for the student and an instrument of perception for the teacher." (259)

So far, however, experimental evidence has not demonstrated that discussion has a consistently greater impact on students' beliefs, values or behavior than more didactic methods of teaching. Admittedly, the issue does not lend itself easily to proof. But several carefully controlled studies have found very little difference between either the academic or the value outcomes of discussion-taught and other classes under comparable conditions.

At Michigan, elementary psychology classes matched for academic ability were taught by three methods—recitation, discussion and tutorial. (258) Each instructor in the experiment used all three methods, and in applying the methods tried to follow a common pattern, so as to hold the personal characteristics of instruction as constant as possible. This result was evidently obtained to a large degree, as no marked differences in outcome distinguished the students of any one instructor.

By and large, *no differences* in educational outcomes emerged as between the three methods. Before-and-after tests measured, in addition to factual learning, such qualities as the ability to apply learning to aid the student's understanding of human behavior in his everyday life, increased skill in formulating conclusions and evaluating them, awareness of the adaptability of human nature, and an attitude of understanding toward individual differences. Nothing in the results encouraged hope that discussion (or the even more individualized "tutorial" approach) was superior in reducing misconceptions about human behavior, developing less rigid conceptions of the roles of parents and more respect for the child as a person, or stimulating positive attitudes toward the subject of psychology. The few differences which appeared statistically significant favored the *recitation-drill method*. The groups taught by this method tended toward higher academic achievement (at all levels of intelligence) and produced more students who wished to go on with the study of psychology. (258)

The evaluators qualified their findings in several ways. The possibility of delayed reactions was not checked. The teachers who conducted the experimental classes were relatively inexperienced. And the experimental manipulation of the instructional procedure affected only a small segment of the student's learning process: the student's previous classroom experiences both in college and before had emphasized content acquisition; the psychology course was just one among the many he was taking; and even it gave common examinations regardless of the teaching method used. Hence the variations in method, substantial though they were in themselves, amounted to a comparatively small alteration of the total environment.

Nevertheless, the results of this experiment are important, because they appear to confirm the implications of other research along the same lines.[1]

A different type of inquiry, conducted at Chicago, raises the possibility however, that the discussion method may affect the quality of a student's *thinking,* even if it does not leave a distinctive mark on his fundamental conceptions and conduct.

Students were asked to recall what they were thinking about at various points during a class, the proceedings of which had been recorded and then played back to them. This device of "stimulated recall" was shown to produce reliable observations. Content analysis of the students' recollections revealed that during a discussion class a much higher percentage of thinking was relevant to the subject at hand than in a lecture, and more thought was directed at problem solving in contrast to simple comprehension. Students were also more concerned about "being adequate" in discussion. On the other hand, there was a tremendous amount of irrelevant and inadequate thinking during both lecture and discussion, and the variation among classes in amount of relevant thinking was very great, regardless of the method of instruction. (255, 256)

Perhaps the most arresting finding was that the quality and relevance of student's thought bore little relation to his active participation in the discussion. *Covert* participation could be just as effective as *overt,* and teachers could not judge accurately the effectiveness of their students on the basis of overt activity alone. All of which leads the Chicago probers to conclude that a discussion class is still an extremely blunt instrument, though they insist it has tremendous promise in stimulating learning.

The major problem in improving the discussion method as they see it is to reduce the percentage of thoughts which center on the self or on other persons present. To this end they recommend that 1) instruction be student-centered in the sense that the instructor recognize and take account of the anxieties, difficulties and needs of his

[1] C. V. Good. "Colleges and Universities: VIII. Methods of teaching." In W. S. Munroe (Ed.) *Encyclopedia of Educational Research,* pp. 273-278, New York: Macmillan, 1952; also Eglash, (257) Fersh (124).

students, 2) that instruction be instructor-centered, meaning that the instructor organize the educative experiences and bring his competence to bear on his students, 3) that the discussion continually raise problems which are challenging to the students.

The implications of this conclusion seem almost to contradict the emphasis of the "classical" student-centered approach espoused by Rogers and his followers. What students need if this evaluation is accurate is *more* direction, not less, for discussion to function effectively as a teaching technique. Indeed, the desire and need for *direction* on the part of the bulk of American college students seems to run throughout most of the studies of their educational responses.

EDUCATION THROUGH EXPERIENCE—LABORATORY PRACTICES AND THE PROBLEM APPROACH

Some educators have long insisted that the most vital learning requires "doing." Only by building upon personal experiences can teaching induce the fullest intellectual growth, according to this philosophy. And changes in values would depend even more upon students confronting situations and working through problems in which value-issues were at stake. What they learned would then become an integral part of their lives, not just a dangling fragment of quiz-kid knowledge.

This approach is currently taking hold in the field of citizenship education, as an attempt to counteract the widespread apathy of American youth toward public affairs. The Citizenship Education Project of Teachers College, Columbia, is the major program in the field, heavily supported by the Carnegie Corporation. When what it calls "laboratory practices" are introduced in social studies as well as other courses, the Project reports that students' interest in public affairs increases, their judgment on political and social issues matures and their sense of personal involvement in citizenship improves. (263)

In essence, these practices are projects which involve students in some form of political or social action. To secure the official seal of approval, a laboratory practice must meet six criteria: 1) It must deal with a *real* situation of concern to the students, in contrast to "role playing" or a mock situation, 2) it must have *focus*, that is be definite enough in area and time to prevent diffusion of effort or inability to end it before the point of diminishing returns is reached, 3) its *purpose* of citizenship training must be known to both teacher and students, 4) it must involve *democratic values*—students' experience should be directly related to principles which underlie the American tradition of liberty, 5) students must *get information first-hand*, 6) students must *take action* in some way as outcome of their study. (30)

Major emphasis of the Citizenship Education Project has been on work with the public schools, but two groups of colleges have been involved—a group of colleges for teacher education and six liberal arts colleges (Amherst, Wesleyan, Haverford, Colgate, Stephens and Rockford College, Illinois). At the college level, laboratory practices have been fitted into a number of existing courses some of which had previously made provision for laboratory experience. Examples include: Amherst's *"problems" course* in American Civilization and the assignment of students in the course in political parties to do *field work in political campaigns*, Colgate's *"case-study" method* in teaching Urban Sociology, and the course in Population, Haverford's *field-studies* in Sociology and in the introductory course in Social Science and Political Science; and Wesleyan's *internships* and *field surveys* in the Public Affairs seminars in government, economics and sociology. Among specific assignments which qualify as laboratory practices in citizenship education for college students are: a study of community planning for industrial reemployment (Colgate), a survey of local housing (Stephens), promoting a special tax proposal for city improvement (Emporia State Teachers College, Kansas), working in political campaigns and elections and poll-watching, an investigation of community opinion about the federal loyalty and security programs, or the work of Unesco (Wesleyan, Amherst, Haverford), studying the care of dependent children (Rockford), preparing a land-use atlas for a planning commission (Haverford), assessing the operation of fair trade laws (Haverford, Amherst), introducing an honor system in the college (Amherst) and participating in a drive for Red Cross membership and funds (Rockford). (30)

All these programs, it is evident, try to involve the students in an experience which will make some social problem vivid to them and require a substantial investment of effort on their part to do something about it.

The expectation is that this will not only spark a perpetual interest in this particular issue, but excite a general concern for public affairs and a more understanding and responsible approach to them.

How far this really does happen is not clear. At the high school level, evaluation studies conducted by the Citizenship Education Project showed some marked changes in attitudes and interests. One systematic attempt to evaluate the impact of a laboratory practice, utilizing pre- and post-free-response tests on experimental and controlled groups, was undertaken at Amherst with results similar to those observed at the high school level. But reports on the outcomes of the college programs are mainly impressionistic. Certainly *interest* is aroused in courses using these devices (266, 279), and the professors who have utilized the technique have testified as to its effectiveness. (30, 263) But the carry-over into personal behavior and the effect on individual value judgments has not been adequately appraised. The Project's staff, however, as well as most of the cooperating teachers, are convinced that they are on solid ground in assuming that learning is best if it is the product of a *combination* of intellectual and direct experience.

Scattered bits of evidence from other programs tend to support the hope that incorporating carefully designed student experience in their college education can have a considerable influence upon their values. For many years Toledo University required a course in "Effective Citizenship," which was originated by Professor O. Garfield Jones. In it every student makes a precinct survey and predicts how that precinct will vote in the next election. Part of the student's grade depends on the accuracy of his prediction. A 100% canvass of graduates who had taken the course twenty years before indicated a lasting effect on their political behavior. Over 95% were registered voters and over 92% had voted in the 1950 state election. A particular factor apparently contributed to an almost perfect voting record for the classes which graduated in 1930 and 1931. As students they had participated along with faculty in a house-to-house canvass and manned the polls on election day in order to secure approval of a bond issue to buy a new campus and erect buildings for the university. Professor Jones concludes that "in the process of persuading the Toledo electorate to vote for the university bond issue in 1928, these students did an even better job of convincing themselves of the importance of voting." (129)

This view is passionately expressed in a comprehensive evaluation of the impact of college on political participation made for the Citizenship Clearing House by Thomas and Doris Reed. They single out personal political experience as the factor above all which distinguishes an effective course from ineffective ones, in this regard, and they denounce most contemporary offerings in social science, especially at the introductory level, as totally useless in the preparation of college men and women for citizenship. (35, 36)

On fronts other than political participation (which may be questioned as an adequate criterion of citizenship in the fullest sense) personal student experience has also heightened the impact of teaching on values. Antioch students uniformly recognize as the most meaningful part of their education the "cooperative study program" in which they intersperse terms of academic study with full-time employment on jobs chosen to advance their personal growth as well as contribute to vocational development. The important outcomes of other off-campus educational programs such as supervised foreign study and travel, or work camps have been verified. (26, 328) Experimental studies of the means of persuasion and communication also attest to the important effect of vivid experience in learning, particularly at the point of forming or modifying a person's beliefs and standards of conduct. (128, 325)

The practical difficulties of working such activities into the educational process are very great, especially in the general part of the curriculum where large numbers of students are involved. For the essence of a potent "laboratory practice" in citizenship, a creative "work camp," a meaningful experiment in international living, a stimulating "work-study" curriculum or even a well-conceived field study is that each student personally engages in the action. Vicarious experience does not deliver the same punch, even though "role-playing" techniques in the classroom and the analysis of challenging case studies and problem situations do arouse more interest in a course.

Real value-laden experiences normally must be secured outside the classroom, and often outside the campus. At most institutions, this automatically rules them out as integral features of a curriculum. Scheduling complexities defy solution, even if the ingenuity of the faculty is sufficient to devise enough significant projects to go around.

Nevertheless, those institutions which have been able to build such experiences into their course of study, or to organize aspects of campus life in such a way that their value-implications carry over into the classroom, have usually had an unmistakable influence on their students.

6

The Peculiar Potency of Some Colleges

Previous sections of this report have questioned whether the curriculum, the instructor or the methods of teaching had much independent force in the value-formation process. But a look at whole colleges rather than just a selection of courses, or other educational influences in isolation, reveals that sometimes a combination of factors can produce a distinctive institutional atmosphere, a "climate of values," in which students *are* decisively influenced.

The incoming student is quick to sense "what goes" on his particular campus. He tends to follow along in the groove he finds, and in short order the pattern of his beliefs and attitudes comes to bear the stamp of his institution. Individual differences among students remain but the range of the differences varies from place to place. No doubt, institutional atmosphere is modified somewhat by the incoming flow of new students and the attitudes they bring with them. It isn't, in other words, a static phenomenon. But there is a self-perpetuating force at work also. Many students (or their parents) are attracted to a place whose atmosphere they expect to be congenial to their previous tastes.

A Record of Liberalism

Certain colleges are clearly more "liberal" in social philosophy. A broad measure of difference among institutions in this regard is the average score of their student bodies on the ACE Inventory of Beliefs. On a scale of 120, a difference of almost 20 points separated the

99

lowest scoring sample from the highest when the test was given in 1951-1952. But what is of even greater significance, the scores at two of the institutions were unusually high while the rest were all pretty much alike. Because of some variations in the conditions under which the test was given one cannot be sure how reliable these differences are, but the spread is so great in the case of the top two that one can presume these student bodies do have a significantly more "liberal" disposition than the others. On a post-test, administered about a year after the first survey (but not with the same students at all places), there is some change in the distribution. Students at two other institutions now join the markedly liberal group, reflecting a shift of point of view during college much larger than at most of the other places. (See Chapter II, table of "Changes in Student Dogmatism During College.")

Antioch students were by far the most liberal on this survey, not only when they entered college but even more so by the time they had completed the freshman year. They had acquired greater tolerance of others—confidence in the capacity of persons to manage their social relations—skepticism concerning personal or national superiority and capacity for leadership—respect for non-conformity—and autonomy of religious conviction. Summed up, Antioch's impact on an already liberally-disposed group is to make it outstandingly "humanist." (280, 281)

Similar changes in attitudes, only of even greater magnitude, are the normal experience at Bennington and Sarah Lawrence where most of the students come from homes of wealth and status and start with quite a conservative outlook on social and economic issues. (85,88)

Personality Differences

Differences among colleges have also been measured in terms of dominant personality characteristics of their student bodies.

Recent analyses, based on experimental use of a modified form of the Inventory of Beliefs, have distinguished some student bodies which are more "rationalist" than others, some more "authoritarian," and some which include a large segment of "anti-authoritarians." (15)

In these studies, student personality types were identified by their rejection or acceptance of various kinds of stereotypes. "S" subjects or *authoritarian stereopaths* accept statements which are tradionalist, ethnocentric, or stress authority and obedience in human relations; they reject statements of an opposite point of view. "N" subjects reverse the pattern, rejecting authoritarian statements and accepting their opposites; they are dogmatically *anti-authoritarian*. "R" students, or *rationalists*, tend to reject all kinds of stereotypes regardless of substance or slant. In addition some persons, especially at the high school level, tend to accept all kinds of stereotypes regardless of content, and even if clearly contradictory in substance. This makes them *irrationalists*—at the other extreme from the "R's."

The following breakdown shows the different proportions of each type of student at various colleges:

	S	N	R	I	Unclassified	Total %	n
High Schools	29	1	14	19	37	100	210
Military Academy	26	2	35	0	37	100	299
NE College	19	4	27	4	46	100	2756
S College	12	4	24	12	48	100	73
MW College	8	18	44	0	30	100	636
Homosexuals	8	26	31	4	31	100	72
Liberal Seminary	5	45	50	0	0	100	29
Group Dynamicists	2	26	60	0	11	100	297
NW College	2	27	56	0	14	100	390

The following breakdown[1] shows the percentage of various student bodies who scored below 50 on the "S-N continuum" thus placing them on the "authoritarian side" and the percentage who scored above 50 on the "I-R continuum," thus qualifying as at least modestly "rationalist."

	Below 50 On S-N	Above 50 On I-R	No. Cases
Chicago	38%	92%	418
Fisk	73	65	73
Reed	16	98	390
Shimer (Ill.)	36	96	67
Syracuse freshmen fall, 1954	71	76	1844
Syracuse freshmen fall, 1955 (Liberal Arts only)	73	82	909
West Point entering class, 1952	82	90	299

[1] Professor Stern is not responsible for this last analysis, though it is based on the data he gathered.

These data confirm the general reputation of the Reed College (Oregon) student body as both highly "rational" and "anti-authoritarian," while West Point cadets obviously have a strong authoritarian contingent but mixed with a high proportion of rationalists. Syracuse freshmen are like West Point in that a large proportion are inclined to accept the authoritarian stereotypes; but not so large a proportion are rationalist. Chicago students are not unlike Reed's in their rationalism but a larger proportion agree with authoritarian concepts, which perhaps would surprise the *Chicago Tribune*.

The importance of institutional differences in student personality is one of the major tentative conclusions of another and exhaustive analysis, still in process under the Department of Psychiatry at Harvard Medical School. (286) Perceptions and values of students at one Eastern private university were found to differ in many significant respects from comparable students at another Eastern private university (most of whom were commuters). The disparity between student bodies is attributed first to selective factors operating to limit the kind of student admitted to the institutions; and second to a process of "acculturation" which causes students to retreat from extremes and to conform to the institutional climate as they go through college. The latter explanation is buttressed by the fact that the characteristics of upperclassmen were found to differ substantially in each institution from those of the freshmen. (286)

Other evidences of personality differences between student bodies appear in a test of values for introspection given to random samples of entering freshmen at a state university and a private university. In one group a markedly larger number of students demonstrated a high introspective quality. (291)

DISTINCTIVE VALUE-PROFILES

Institutional characteristics have also been demonstrated on the Allport-Vernon Study of Values, over the last twenty years, even though the students at most institutions tend to have, as previously reported, quite similar patterns of value.

The Theoretical Value: Bennington and Reed students had a markedly *higher theoretical value* than others. (This undoubtedly ties in with Stern's profile of Reed's "rationalism.")

The Aesthetic Value: Bennington and Reed students were also significantly *superior in aesthetic value* than those at other institutions surveyed. American International (Springfield) students were much lower in this respect

The Religious Value: Bennington and C.C.N.Y. students had a *much lower* than general appreciation of religious values; students at Southern institutions a *much higher* appreciation

The Economic, Political, and Social Values: The range of institutional differences is not great in regard to these values. Reed men, however, on a pre-war study, appeared much less concerned with the securing of material satisfactions and power (low economic and political values) which tends to corroborate the distinctive anti-authoritarian trait obtained by Stern's more recent study.

The more substantial differences among institutions are starred in the table below.

The distinctive pattern of values at some institutions is most clearly shown by data from the Cornell Values survey. Students' attitudes towards religion, their political and economic philosophy, the extent of their tolerance, their appreciation for college, and even some of their personality traits seem quite clearly to identify a special "climate" at Harvard, Wesleyan, Texas, and North Carolina.

Harvard—Personal autonomy and the open mind

Harvard undergraduates exhibit an unusual degree of respect for individualism, and tolerance. They tend to be liberal in economics, and sophisticated but not cynical about politics. They are less faithful in religious practice and less orthodox in religious belief than students generally. A larger proportion than elsewhere crave creativity rather than security in their occupations. They have high regard for their college education and they do not cheat.

Wesleyan—Home of the community-minded

In many respects, Wesleyan students' values are akin to Harvard's. They are tolerant, both of other races and of political non-conformists. They share a similar high regard for college, and particularly for a liberal arts education. Cheating is taboo, as at Harvard. They both rank high in political knowledge (but Wesleyan students are somewhat more conservative in political and economic philosophy). Their attitudes toward military service and the armed forces are, like

TABLE 20: Institutional Differences on the Allport-Vernon
Study of Values

(*Original scale*)	Theor.	Econ.	Aesth.	Social	Pol	Relig
Norm (Allport & Cantril) (1933) (103)						
Men	30.8	32.0	27.0	29.7	32.1	28.0
Women	27.7	27.0	33.0	31.6	27.9	33.3
Bennington seniors (85)						
Women	35.7*	27.5	36.7*	32.1	25.1	22.7*
Reed-Men (113)	34.4*	26.2*	32.1*	31.5	26.6*	28.2
Women	30.1*	26.1	35.9*	31.8	24.5	29.9
Springfield College (71)						
1939	29.9	29.6	22.2*	30.9	32.9	35.0*
(*Revised scale*)						
Norm (Allport, Vernon, Lindzey, 1951) (310)						
Men	43.3	42.1	37.2	37.7	42.7	37.0
Women	36.4	38.8	42.2	41.2	38.1	43.2
Springfield College						
Men	43.5	43.1	32.9*	36.6	43.0	40.9
Women	38.9	38.7	40.7	40.7	38.4	42.5
George Peabody						
Men	43.2	41.9	35.9	37.7	40.3	41.0*
Women	35.7	38.6	41.8	40.4	36.9	46.6*
C.C.N.Y						
Men	45.6	39.5	42.0	39.7	43.1	30.1*
Women	42.6	39.3	45.8	42.7	38.7	31.0*
Harvard Men	44.1	40.1	40.6	38.1	42.6	34.4
Radcliffe Women	38.6	32.8*	48.1	44.0	36.5	40.0
Ohio State						
Men	40.9	45.1	34.5	36.9	43.3	39.2
Women	33.7	41.1	40.0	41.8	39.2	44.0
Southwestern at Memphis (114)						
Men	40.7	38.5	36.0	35.9	41.2	47.7*
Women	34.5	35.4	42.8	39.1	36.6	51.5*
Woman's College, North Carolina	34.8	39.3	40.6	39.6	38.0	47.7*

Harvard's, more unfavorable than elsewhere. (6)

But Wesleyan has something which makes its total value climate different—an unusual element of "community-mindedness"—an amalgam of moral purposefulness, concern for civic affairs and group-consciousness. This all seems to go along with a strong religious motivation.

A higher percentage of students at Wesleyan than at any other college consider that:

1) the ideal university's most important educational goal should be to "help develop your moral capacities, ethical standards and values." (17%)

2) the most important requirements of an ideal job would be to "give me an opportunity to help others." (15%)

3) one of the three activities expected to give the most satisfaction in life would be "participation as a citizen in the affairs of your community." (23%)

A very large number (57%) believe development of interest in community and world problems should be *a* major educational goal.

The Wesleyan student body is more religiously oriented than any except those in the south, and is by all odds the most sensitive to religious influences during college (even in comparison with Cornell, which has a reputation for a powerful religious atmosphere.) Half of the students feel that they have come to value religion more since coming to college (as against only 16% who consider that they value it less).

Wesleyan students also have an extraordinary degree of group-consciousness—as applied to family, college, fraternity, church, and nationality. Whereas at other institutions, a considerable body of students may show a strong attachment to one or two of these groups, a large or near majority of Wesleyan men go to the extent of feeling

TABLE 21: Group-Consciousness
(% who feel the group has its own personality—Cornell survey)

	Wes.	Har.	N.C.	Texas	Total
Your Family	55	45	53	44	47
Your College	63	63	57	44	52
Your Fraternity	59	10	35	25	27
Your Church or religion	46	35	47	43	38
Your Nationality	41	32	40	33	32

that every one of them "has its own personality, something over and above the individual members in it."

Seniors show the imprint of community-mindedness more than freshmen, indicating that the college itself has had something to do with creating the "climate." (116) This inference is also warranted because a growth of concern for human relations and public affairs is so untypical of the evolution of student values elsewhere. Apparently the touch of an institution's special influence has been felt—with administration, faculty, curriculum and established tradition all paying steady homage to the civic virtues.

North Carolina and Texas—Strongholds of conformity

On a wide gamut of values, students at these two southern universities stand at the extreme of orthodoxy and conservatism. Religiously, they are the most devout in practice and the most doctrinal in belief. Their political and economic philosophy is the most to the right. More than students in other parts of the country they favor repression of "dangerous" and "radical" views. They tend to have a more cynical view of government and politics. There is naturally more racial prejudice. Security looms more important in considering requirements of the ideal job. Discipline is more highly valued in the rearing of children. These contrasts are obvious in the table of institutional differences.

At North Carolina, however, students are much more satisfied with college education than at Texas and apparently have greater respect for intellectual endeavor and independence. One index of this difference is the cheating record—almost three times greater at Texas.

Haverford—School for leaders

The outlook on the future of Haverford freshmen is similar in many respects to that of the Harvard and Miami men whose "Autobiographies to 2000 A. D." were gathered in the Gillespie-Allport study. (11, 184) They have the same "strong family frame of reference," recognition of a religious need, respect for conventional moral virtues, belief in racial equality, advocacy of internationalist solutions to world problems and confidence in being able to determine their destiny themselves regardless of external circumstances. But as at Wesleyan, there are points of difference which tend to create a climate of its own.

TABLE 22: Institutional Differences on the Cornell Survey

(Items starred are significantly different from the average of all institutions, at a level of confidence of .01 or less)

	Percentage agreeing at				
	Har-vard	Wes-leyan	All Col-leges	North Caro-lina	Tex-as
Tolerance					
It's unwise to give people with dangerous social and economic viewpoints a chance to be elected	25*	34	41	59*	53*
Steps should be taken right away to outlaw the Communist Party	22*	24*	35	51*	55*
If you refuse to support your government in a war you shouldn't continue to live in a country	26*	22*	32	37	42*
Generally speaking Negroes are lazy and ignorant	10*	14	17	44*	31*
The Federal Government should require all employers to hire people without regard to their race, religion, color or nationality	60*	52	48	26*	34*
Public Philosophy					
Democracy depends fundamentally on the existence of free business enterprise	45*	61	62	71*	70*
Government planning almost inevitably results in the loss of essential liberties and freedom	23*	20	31	39*	36*
The "welfare state" tends to destroy individual initiative	47*	52	60	63	60
If people knew what was really going on in high places, it would blow the lid off things	23*	29*	37	45*	46*

TABLE 22: Institutional Differences on the Cornell Survey—*Continued*

	Har-vard	Wes-leyan	Percentage agreeing at All Col-leges	North Caro-lina	Tex-as
Religion					
Personally feel need to believe in some sort of religious faith or personal philosophy	69*	83	78	89*	88*
Attend religious service—never or almost never	33*	14*	24	9*	15*
I personally value religion *more* since I came to college	30	49*	32	34	33
less	22*	16	16	12*	14*
Belief in Divine God, Creator of Universe, etc.	30*	43	44	68*	62*
Naturalist, agnostic, or atheist	32*	21	24	14*	13*
Appreciation of college					
My own university is doing a very good job in fulfilling educational goals I consider important	54*	41*	33	30	17*
I think most college students would cheat on an exam if they were sure of not being caught	23*	19*	32	33	46*
I used crib notes or copied in an examination while at college —somewhat or much more than once	5*	5*	19	11*	27*
American colleges today should place more emphasis on teaching religious values	16*	22	22	33*	30*
American colleges today should place more emphasis on teaching American ideals and values	17*	20	31	29	41*
My college has its own personality, something over and above the individual members in it	63*	63*	52	57	44*

TABLE 22: Institutional Differences on the Cornell Survey—*Continued*

	Har-vard	Wes-leyan	All Col-leges	North Caro-lina	Tex-as
			Percentage agreeing at		
Human relations					
These days parents aren't strict enough with their children	31*	43	44	51*	57*
It's who you know more than what you know that counts these days	18*	23*	30	41*	39*
Personality					
Very important, personally, to get ahead in life	49	53	51	74*	65*
Important to have plans for future clearly known in advance	24*	24*	32	44*	39*
Very important to be well liked by different kinds of people	37*	45	45	62*	53*
Qualifications of the ideal job					
The most important requirement is: Permit me to be creative and original	16*	10	10	5*	8
Enable me to look forward to a stable, secure future	16*	20	24	35*	27
Give me an opportunity to be helpful to others	10	15*	9	13*	9

Haverford students appear obsessed with a success mania in contrast to the others, whose lack of competitiveness and personal ambition so forcibly struck Gillespie and Allport that they wondered whether the American character had undergone a basic alteration. In this regard, Haverford can claim custody of the original American species. Well over half the students crave to be "leaders," "important," "successful," "outstanding," "renowned," "famous" in their careers. They even specify that they want their children to be "successful," and that they would like to make a contribution to society which "would be remembered." Only one student was satisfied to state that he'd like to "have a good job and do it well" or anything so singularly unexceptional. Perhaps Haverford is the last haven for the frontiersman and the iron buccaneer. Among the class of '56 at any rate, there was one who would build the greatest road in the world, another whose greatest pride would lie in reorganizing a defunct organization, a boy who longed to operate successfully an independent railroad and two who wanted to get to the moon.

Part of this drive for leadership spills over into social and civic concerns, so that the student body as a whole is markedly less "privatistic" and more interested in social problems than its Harvard or Miami counterparts. As compared with 15% of the Harvard undergraduates who evinced interest in social problems, a good third of the Haverford group acknowledged at least verbally their respect for activities devoted to the betterment of mankind. Whereas only 2% of the original sample indicated readiness to include philanthropy among the objects for which they would spend a windfall, 16% of the Haverford freshmen listed charity or causes as something for which they would give at least some money. Rather more of the Haverford group (11% instead of 3%) ranked activity in civic affairs high among the accomplishments of which they would be proud. As many as 25% would consider some form of service to the world, through or outside of government, as one of the two worthiest achievements they could contemplate. As between local activities, and the national or international scene, the Haverford students are much more attracted by the latter; whereas to the extent that the students at Harvard and Miami are civic-conscious at all, they tend to express their interest at the local level.

One should not exaggerate the extent or depth of Haverford's public-spiritedness, however. By far the majority of students remain true to the "new" American character—preoccupied with life in a personal world, apart from any of the social communities surrounding them. They are savers and investors—for their own or their immediate family's gain. A fair number are spenders—also for their own or their family's personal enjoyment. And only a few appear greatly concerned lest they develop a reputation for inadequate citizenship or social apathy. (184)

Toward the service of mankind

A few institutions have apparently been able to arouse the selfless motivations of an unusual number of their students, and propel them towards values which stress the well-being of others. This accomplishment is especially significant because it runs against the prevailing current.

At Springfield College, students' love of people and altruism (the "social value" on the Allport-Vernon Study of Values) increased during their stay so that this became *the pre-eminent value for seniors*. Such a result is unique among the institutions for which this type of data is available. As freshmen, these students did not start with any greater than average degree of social sensitivity. What happened to their values can hardly be accounted for apart from their particular college experience.

A study of students who dropped out reinforces this conclusion. Those who left had motivations which were incompatible with the cultural climate on the campus. Their social motivation was weaker than others, their aspiration for material gain and for power (the "economic" and "political" values) was inordinately strong compared with their fellow students who stayed. The college influence was apparently so potent that they could not "take it". (71)

These results will not surprise those who know that Springfield College directs a large part of its program towards the training of social workers, YMCA secretaries, physical education directors and other types of personnel for service and welfare activities. It is also a center of missionary interest and preparation.

TABLE 23: The Service–Orientation at Springfield College
(Changes on the Allport-Vernon Study of Values) (71)

	Social Value		Economic Value	
	Fresh men	Sen iors	Fresh men	Sen iors
Physical Education majors	30.9	35.0	29.4	27.9
Social Science majors	32.5	37.3	29.0	24.4

The same kind of special institutional influence occurs at Macalester, a Presbyterian-affiliated college with a strong commitment to public and humanitarian service running through administration, faculty and both curricular and extra-curricular programs. Here, a very large number of students undergo a change of vocational direction during college—from business, farming, or the professions to some type of altruistic human welfare activity. Background and outlook of the entering freshmen is sufficiently conventional that one would not expect them to veer so sharply into "self-less" occupations. It is the institution which apparently triggers a new sense of perspective and a critical reappraisal by the student of what shall be his overriding values. Within such a live institutional atmosphere, the curriculum can become unusually influential. The introductory courses in History and Political Science at Macalester spark an extraordinary sense of social and political responsibility, arouse keen interest in civic and political affairs (not only in the immediate community but in the world at large), influence the choice of service vocations, and generally alert students to the duties of "Christian citizenship." The immediate stimulus to these value changes may really be the instructors rather than the particular type of course or curriculum. They seem to acquire a new potency under such institutional conditions.[2]

Religious motivation—the church college's safe shelter

Students at denominational colleges tend to espouse religiously-oriented life goals more than do students generally. "Serving God" was the highest ranked life goal in a survey in 1942-1943 conducted mainly among church-affiliated colleges. By contrast, living for pleasure of the moment, seeking power and control over people, and "survival" were the lowest ranked goals.

However, one can hardly attribute this orientation to institutional influences alone. An unusually large proportion of the students admitted to such colleges are already conditioned by family and church training to hold such views. The college's role then was merely to reinforce the pattern and protect the student's values from change. This result was apparently accomplished at those institutions which joined in the survey of Life Goals. (4) Denominational colleges seem to have comparatively little *positive* effect on students' religious views. Of several hundred teachers at church-related colleges, few could recall that their own religious development had been appreciably

[2] Further evidence of the influence of institutional ideals on students' life goals is reported in Dunkel. (4)

affected by college experience, whether or not it had included compulsory chapel, required courses in religion and Bible and the other features common to institutions with a strong religious commitment. (231) By contrast, half of the students at Wesleyan (a non-sectarian institution despite its name) felt that they personally had come to a higher valuation of religion during college. Against this standard church colleges can claim no specially potent role in the business of strengthening and enlightening their students' religious perceptions.

Public vs. Private institutions—a difference in student educational goals

No consistent pattern of student values distinguishes publicly supported universities from the private campuses except in one regard— the educational goal which students consider most important. The issue of vocationalism as against general education cuts sharply along the lines of institutional administration in the Cornell survey. At public institutions, students divided about equally in espousing education for a career or a basic general education. But at Harvard,

TABLE 24: Vocational Training Vs. General Education
(Cornell Survey)

Percentage of students who consider the most important educational goal of the ideal college or university to be:

(1)—Provide vocational training; develop skills and techniques directly applicable to your career

(2)—Provide a basic general education and appreciation of ideas

	(1)	(2)
Public institutions:		
UCLA	37	32
Cornell	35	32
Michigan	38	32
North Carolina	36	26
Texas	39	25
Wayne	45	21
Private:		
Dartmouth	12	47
Harvard	15	48
Wesleyan	14	47
Yale	11	52

Wesleyan, Yale, and Dartmouth students chose general education almost four to one over vocational training as the most important goal.

THE NATURE OF THE INSTITUTIONAL THRUST

Just what causes differences in values to emerge among student bodies and some colleges to acquire a distinctive character is still quite uncertain. Intensive studies of institutional influences are rare and to isolate what happens at a particular college from other possible factors is very difficult.

For instance, the "southerness" of students surely accounts for most of the differences noted at Texas and North Carolina rather than any special influence of those institutions.

"Urban-ness" may tend to encourage a more secular and nonreligious atmosphere at such institutions as Wayne and UCLA. (These institutions were significantly different in this regard on the Cornell survey.)

The working class background of many students at Wayne probably alters their outlook on economic questions and makes security a more important life goal than is generally true. It may also have affected their responsiveness to military service at the time of the Korean war, increasing their reluctance to serve because of the greater disruptions of personal and family security it would cause. (6)

A college's admissions policy or reputation often selects or attracts students who are "typed" with a certain outlook or pattern of values before they ever enter. This is probably responsible for the extra "religiousness" of students at many church-related colleges. It evidently also has something to do with producing Harvard's unique climate of mind and values. (286)

Where, however, there is evidence that changes in student values occur between freshman and senior years and these changes are not typical of the general trend over the country, one may reasonably infer that the students are responding to the influence of their own campus. The process of "acculturation" is at work.

Newcomb's analysis of personality and social change at Bennington College remains a unique case study of this kind of transformation of students' values (84, 85), though his explanation of the change is widely supported by other evidence from institutions very different in character. (10, 201, 286) At Bennington, many girls reversed the

basic beliefs current in their social and family milieus, going far beyond the usual student experience at other colleges. The most striking
of these changes was the rather common rejection of political-eco-
nomic-social conservatism. The point of view acquired by many of
these girls could properly have been described as "radical" in the late
1930's, and even now is well to the left of the general student population.

Newcomb believes that these changes resulted from the very strong
impulse to conform to what fellow-students, and particularly the student leaders in the college community, considered good and proper.
They were willing to become very different from their family and the
world outside, in order not to differ from what was approved in their
own immediate community. In this process, faculty played a part. Because they ranked high in status and influence among students, and
tended to be much less conservative, they reinforced the prestige of
those "liberal" values which the student leadership had espoused.
Taken as a whole, the college community acting more or less uncon-
sciously, defined a limited number of roles—channels of behavior and
approved sets of attitudes—which were open to students if they wished
to succeed and gain the esteem of their associates.

It may be that the liberal arts private college, with a sense of a
special educational mission, is more likely to have a potent influence
on student values than public institutions. Even if further evidence
supports such a conclusion, however, the matter cannot be left here.
For the building of such a distinctive institution is a subtle and
rather unpredictable process, and at best there will not be many to
go around. The fate of the values of the mass of students rests with
the public institutions.

If one grants that the odds at a mammoth state institution which
has to accommodate virtually every high school graduate who has a
yen for a degree are heavily against its exerting a significant educational impact on students' values, what can be done to maximize the
effect it can have in this regard? In what direction should its efforts
strive? Are there means by which individualization can be encouraged
even in these institutions, both in the content of their curriculum
and in instruction? Does a general education emphasis in such circumstances tend to negate what limited opportunity there may be
to diversify, and to develop "atmosphere"—or perhaps a lot of separate

atmospheres—at the institution? In the pursuit of good social values for everyone, does general education, conducted for a massive college population, undermine the core value, that is, the capacity of a person himself to choose his values and thereby *be* a person?

In many ways, *diversity*—among and within colleges—is the most precious feature of the American educational environment, and the secret of what value-outcomes can be credited to educational influences. It keeps open the possibility that differences among individuals in insight, personality and value judgments can be perpetuated. If it is true that institutional atmosphere has a normative impact on students, then a narrowing of institutional diversity would have the effect of compressing into a common mold whatever individuality is left after students pass through eighteen years of the American nurturing process, including their twelve years of public school education.

7

Student Personality—A Filter of Educational Values

Now comes the question of individual differences in the response of students to their college education. Educational influences have so far been appraised in terms of their impact on group values—the relative numbers of students at various institutions who have believed or behaved in a similar fashion. But what causes a particular student to change his values in a particular way, while another does not change or changes in a different way? Why does one find that his appreciation for religion increases, and another in an almost identical educational context comes to feel that he values it less? Why does one become a crusader for social reform while another at the same college and exposed to the same influences aspires after personal economic success? However uniform certain values appear among students *en masse*, whether on one campus or many, there are always some persons who deviate—why?

This query, if pursued adequately, would extend far beyond the compass and competence of the present inquiry, and into deep psychological waters. Some of the data studied, however, touch broadly on the significance of various personality factors in determining what students get out of their education, and seem appropriate to include in this report, without any presumption that a comprehensive or balanced representation of research in the field is thereby provided.[1]

[1] Asch (52) and Edgar (201) give useful commentaries on the research in this area.

This evidence suggests that the response of students to education, especially general education, is vitally conditioned by their own personalities. A course or curriculum, a teacher, or even a college as a whole, will affect students differently, depending on what type of persons they are. The educational impact is twisted and re-directed by its collision with a particular student's personality. The personality acts as a filter, allowing only certain elements from the educational process to get through to the student and influence him.

Some of the important components of the personality filter which control educational influences for an individual have been identified as

1) a pragmatic orientation

2) a pattern of conformity behavior

3) "syndromes" of authoritarianism, anti-authoritarianism and rationalism.

These are not discrete phenomena and several are apparently closely interrelated if not actually different aspects of the same basic trait. The concepts, however, each form the point of departure or conclusion for a separate series of experiments or analyses and for the sake of clarity will be considered separately.

A Pragmatic Revolt vs. General Education

A major reason for the failure of some students to respond favorably to a program of general or liberal education has been their obsession with "practical" goals. They are so intent on getting on in the world, that they have no value for learning as such. They are interested only in training which will advance specific vocational or other utilitarian objectives, not in discovering truth about themselves and the universe around them. In the judgment of some psychiatric authorities this type of "pragmatic", as against an "ideistic" orientation has its roots in personality structure. (167, 203)

A special inquiry into the emotional and social adjustment of "Early Admissions Scholars" (students admitted to college before finishing high school in an experiment sponsored by the Fund for the Advancement of Education) (167) found that the educational response not only of the younger students but also of regular students was profoundly affected by deeply laid down values, probably related to early experiences in their families. If the student came from a family where education and intellectual matters were prized and he was not blocked in his identification with his parents, he acquired a high value for education. On the other hand, if this were not the case, the changing values and attitudes at college produced an undue and sometimes excessive demand on the student's emotional resources. To some students the values of the college were so foreign that they could not realistically assess their academic performance. Though failing badly in some of their subjects, they were quite unworried, sure that "everything would come out all right." In contrast, some students with a high value for education would show great concern if for emotional or other reasons they were in academic difficulty. In another type of response, the "pragmatically oriented" student would fight back at his education, refusing to go to class, or at least expressing bitter resentment against his "impractical" courses as a waste of time.

The educational implications of such a fundamental conflict of values between the student and the college he attends are serious. For one thing, this is undoubtedly an important factor in many colleges in causing students to drop out—in some institutions at the fantastic rate of 50% before graduation. The problem is accentuated if students who are vocationally, or pragmatically oriented are having to go through a liberal arts curriculum. The teacher under these circumstances faces very great difficulties because he is trying to transmit values in opposition to the basic bent of the student's personality while healthy psychological development demands some continuity of value systems, according to the specialists who conducted this analysis.

Some ways out of the dilemma may be possible. The report to the Fund for the Advancement of Education stresses the importance of placing "the proper student in the proper school." Liberal arts colleges should be cautious, it holds, about admitting vocationally minded students who have little value for the liberal arts. Better instruments of selection are needed which will determine students' attitudes in this regard and how susceptible to change they are. Better techniques can be devised to teach liberal arts to those not interested in them. It is particularly important for a teacher to understand psychological factors underlying the conflict in values systems between a student and his educational program. He can then facilitate the learning process by providing emotional support to the student, rather than trying directly to exact a response to values which the student doesn't and probably cannot recognize.

THE DISPOSITION TO CONFORM

Some students find it comparatively easy to bring their values into line with views held by those around them. They are flexible, and susceptible to outside influences—educational as well as social. Others tend to resist change to conform to a new group standard. Their personal values are quite rigid, whether they are holding to judgments which they have formed rather independently or to ones inherited from family or some other established source. The nature of the student's response to education, especially in terms of his disposition to reevaluate attitudes and behavioral standards, is related to this quality, which in turn reflects general characteristics of personality.

Newcomb's analysis of the various responses of Bennington students to the liberal atmosphere of the college community brought out these factors which seemed to determine who would conform and who would not. (85) First was the kind of adjustment students had made to their parents before they came to college. Those who had become independent of their parents found no great obstacle in accepting college attitudes which differed from their parents'. But overdependence on parents prevented them from changing their attitudes to conform to the college community. Either their tie to their parents was so all-absorbing that the college influence was scarcely felt, or the conflict between parents and college standards produced such intolerable tension that they withdrew.

A second factor was the sense of personal adequacy which students felt in their relations with others of their own age. Those unable to achieve goals of prestige and leadership which they had set for themselves in the community of their peers tended to reject its standards and to find refuge in a more limited social group whose values were more congenial to what they had previously held. In other words they would not conform to the values of a community which they felt had not adequately accepted them (at least in terms of the recognition to which they personally aspired). They *would* conform to a substitute group in which they did feel accepted.

The third factor influencing the student's disposition to conform was his degree of passivity or initiative. The more passive, with fewer social skills and social ambitions, changed their attitudes only to the extent necessary to establish themselves as good respectable citizens in the Bennington college community. The more aggressive and ambitious made a greater than average change in order to gain leadership. These individuals really over-conformed paradoxically as a technique of demonstrating independence, responsibility and the other qualities which might earn them influence and prestige. Conformity to the college's climate of values thus became an instrument in the "struggle for power" on the campus.

What can happen in a classroom as a result of students' disposition to conform or not to conform is illustrated by a personality analysis of students who voluntarily took part—in discussion, raising questions, etc.—in a psychology class at a small liberal arts college. (143) In comparison with those who only spoke when they had to, the active participants were significantly more self-confident, ascendant, socially independent, socially aggressive, intelligent, critical, and informed— though they had *no more real interest* in the course than the non-participants. But whereas at Bennington this type of behavior would have been ultra-conforming and marked these students as leaders on the campus, at this college the opposite was apparently true. Taking part in class was *non*-conforming behavior (at least from the point of view of the student body which one gathers did not particularly honor "braininess"). An indication of this is seen in the fact that significantly more non-fraternity than fraternity students voluntarily participated. Here then were students full of ambition and initiative but who had failed to gain leadership on a campus-wide basis. They rejected the campus norm—in this case, intellectual passivity—and adopted instead an opposite pattern of conduct, one which undoubtedly pleased the faculty more.

Whether a particular student will respond actively to *educational* influences, thus depends first on whether his attachments, aspirations and social experiences have made him a conforming personality, and second on whether the college has captured control of the campus standards of conformity, and made *its* values the ones by which the student community measures success and acceptability.

a) If the college has succeeded in getting the values it cherishes (educational and otherwise) generally accepted as the major standard of achievement *within* the student body (as at Bennington), then *two groups of conformists will be responsive to its influence*—those who are successful aspirants for leadership and those who are adaptive followers. Under these circumstances the independent souls who fell short of their goals of leadership would tend to rebel against the established educational process and the college values and find unacceptable ways in which to demonstrate their independence (perhaps "living it up").

b) But if the college's educational goals and value standards are secondary to some other standard in the unwritten code of student achievement, the reverse is likely to be true. The conformists will be unresponsive to the educational stimuli, while only the frustrated bidders for leadership will turn avidly to educational accomplishment as a means of rebellion against the community which did not accept and reward them.

The extreme importance of matching student personality and the institutional climate of values is obvious. A passive, acceptant, following type of student will hardly develop mature values if he or she lands in a university where athletic prowess, social popularity, smart dress or family name and income are the main things that count among students. Nor will the "big man" go far towards *intellectual* independence and a positive ethic in an atmosphere where his drive and leadership will be spent on achieving physical gratifications. On the other hand, this might be just the place to bring out the most creative intellectual endeavor and critical judgment of values on the part of a student with active ambition but who for one reason or another cannot become a social success or athletic hero. To salvage the intellectual and moral potentials of the first two groups (the followers and the success students), however, an institution with a firmly implanted and pervasive climate of values is called for. Unfortunately, the number of such institutions is limited while the students who need this kind of environment are legion.[2]

The "Authoritarian Personality" as a College Student

In the previous chapter, one of the important differences noted among colleges was in the prevailing personality characteristics of their student bodies. A principal basis of distinction was the propor-

[2] The intensive experimental studies of Crutchfield and Asch demonstrate in detail varying degrees of conformity behavior and some of the corresponding personality traits. (52)

tion of students who could be identified by various traits and attitudes as "authoritarian," "rationalist," or "anti-authoritarian." Research in progress indicates that such differences in personality have a real bearing upon the way particular students respond to their education and consequently what its impact is upon their values.

The claim, advanced originally in a pioneer study by a team of California psychologists and psychiatrists, that some persons have acquired a coherent, well-defined body of attitudes, traits and values which constitute an "authoritarian" type of personality, has been hotly disputed on a variety of grounds. Nevertheless, several other explorations of personality types have come to conclusions remarkably similar. (15, 50, 286, 303, 306) The term "authoritarian" is unfortunate because of its ideological connotations. "Rigid," "dogmatic," "prejudiced," "stereopathic" are alternative labels used to describe essentially the same phenomenon. There is some evidence that the psychiatric diagnosis of a "compulsive-neurotic" is akin to, though probably a narrower and more specific form of, the authoritarian personality. (286)

The studies by Stern and his associates at Chicago, Syracuse and elsewhere have demonstrated a striking consistency between the *beliefs* and the *conduct* of students of the authoritarian or stereopath type. Scores on the ACE Inventory of Beliefs which indicate the extent to which persons reject various kinds of stereotypes correlate very significantly with such factors as religious affiliation, choice of vocation, psycho-diagnostic assessment and other indices of personality. For instance, in a quite diversified sampling of students,

Emotional instability was more frequently noted among students who had low scores, i.e. accepted the authoritarian-slanted stereotypes.

These students' stated purpose in coming to college reflected the influence of prestige associated with the institution or a view of education as the basis for future financial security.

Two-thirds of such students chose "instrumental" vocations (engineering, medicine, business administration, etc.) in contrast to non-authoritarians, three-fourths of whom chose "consummatory" vocations (teaching, the arts, social service, etc.)

Three-fourths of the authoritarians belonged to orthodox, fundamentalist or evangelical churches; three-fourths of the non-authoritarians were members of liberal denominations or had no religious affiliation.

A separate study at Antioch identified specific forms of conduct and outlook in college which were characteristic of those who scored low on the Inventory of Beliefs, in contrast to those who scored high. (281) Among the significant associations were:

1) Low scorers (the more "authoritarian") were less interested in community participation.
2) They tended to see no excuses for handing papers in late, criticized those who did hand them in late.
3) They attached more importance to neatness.
4) They emphasized dress.
5) They regarded common room rules as legitimate and to be obeyed.
6) They denied the existence of homosexuality or were embarrassed by discussion of it. High scorers accepted homosexuals as people and the better informed among them saw some possibility of a solution, perhaps in terms of counseling.
7) The low group thought of moral laxity as associated with sex and drinking; high group asked for a definition of "laxity."

Further aspects of student personality are under intense observations by Funkenstein and a team at the Harvard Medical School's Department of Psychiatry. They have examined a representative cross-section of upperclassmen in an Eastern private university in a lengthy sequence of interviews, and by a battery of tests as well as laboratory stress experiments. The battery included tests of ethnocentrism, traditional family ideology, religious conventionalism and the "F-scale" of authoritarianism; also the Brownfain self-concept test, a social attitudes questionnaire and projective tests such as the Rorschach and Thematic Apperception Tests. Although the study was chiefly oriented around other facets of personality than authoritarianism, let us summarize their findings in this particular area:

The studies were carried out on college juniors. Almost all of these students had non-authoritarian attitudes as measured by these tests. The few students who were relatively high on authoritative attitudes, but not absolutely high, showed the following characteristics:

1) Students who were the most authoritarian were also the most ethnocentric, religiously conventional, attached to a traditional family ideology and politically and economically conservative.
2) Students relatively high on authoritative attitudes, personality wise, showed psychological evidence of rigidity. They were intolerant,

could not accept ambiguities, tended to put blame on persons or factors other than themselves, placed little value on introspection for which they showed little capacity. They were little aware of psychological factors and showed little conscious anxiety or guilt.

3) Those scoring relatively high on authoritative scales see fewer differences between these aspects of their personalities than the low scorers. The students who were least authoritarian had just the opposite traits. They had the capacity to tolerate ambiguities and to shift from one frame of reference to another as indicated on the Brownfain self-concept test. (This asks a person to distinguish between his "best self," his "worst self," his "actual self" and his "social self" or the way in which he thinks others see him.)

4) During the stress experiments, the relatively high authoritarians most often denied expression of emotion and showed marked control. They ascribed their difficulties to factors outside themselves, "extro-punitive."

5) Those scoring relatively high on the authoritarian scales placed little value on reflective thinking, but prized neatness and dependability. The less authoritarian individuals, on the other hand, valued flexibility and self-understanding.

6) The more authoritarian students saw their fathers as both their chief source of authority and as their chief source of affection. The least authoritarian were "Matrists," feeling strong affection towards their mothers and also looking to their mothers as the chief source of authority in the family. The extremely non-authoritarian boys had this ambivalent relationship with their mothers, whereas the extremely authoritarian group had this ambivalent relationship with their fathers. Students without this ambivalent relationship with either parent, in that one parent fulfilled the role of authority and the other the role of affection, although non-authoritarian but not extremely so, had more mature personalities.

It should be emphasized that these personality characteristics accompanying relatively high scorers on an authoritarian scale occurred at one college in upperclassmen. When these tests were repeated in this same college with freshmen and at another college, these same relationships between personality and scores on authoritarian scales were not obtained. These investigators gave as a preliminary interpretation of their data, awaiting further experimentation, that high scores on authoritarian scales have at least two sets of factors associated with them: one is the personality factors, and another social-cultural factors. When a student with high scores on authoritarian scales enters as a freshman into a college, where the majority of students are low scorers, he will soon change to a low score himself, provided the high score on the authoritarian scale does not represent a deeply laid down aspect of his personality. When such high scores do represent deeply laid down aspects of personality, then, even if he enters as a freshman a college with predominantly low scorers, he will fail to change. This probably accounts for the relationship of the findings enumerated above in college juniors where high scores on an authoritarian battery did correlate with personality factors, whereas at the same college in freshmen no score correlations were found. In other words, high scores, on authoritarian scales are in some instances predominantly socially and culturally determined, in others predominantly personality determined. If a student enters a college where attitudes and values differ markedly from his, ability to change is also related to ego strength. This probably accounts for the failure in many instances of other investigators to obtain correlations between high scorers on authoritarian scales and other tests of psychological rigidity. Extensive research is indicated in this area.

These personality differences have a profound effect on educational performance. Most obviously, the authoritarians get lower grades, and the least authoritarian students get higher—especially in humanities and social science courses. The differences in natural science and mathematics have not been statistically significant. (15, 281, 306) The authoritarian-inclined students drop out of college at a much higher rate. (1, 15) They want directive instruction providing clear and explicit explanations of what is expected of them, and preferably objective-type examinations. When the Michigan State Board of Examiners interviewed students to get their opinion about a new type of examination procedure (which would widen the possible choice in multiple choice tests, etc.) the authoritarian students not only opposed any change in the established procedure but often resisted being interviewed about it. They apparently wanted to be told, rather than to be consulted. (287) At Harvard, permissive-type teaching caused some students to experience great emotional strain. They were confused, even angry; whereas under straight lecture and recitation they moved along contentedly. The reverse was the case with some of the more extreme liberals or non-authoritarians. What is influential education for an authoritarian, therefore, frustrates a liberal, and vice versa. (252)

The most careful inquiry to examine the effect of personality structure on a student's educational performance so far observed is an experiment designed and conducted at Syracuse during 1955 by George Stern and Alfred Cope. (146) Freshmen in the basic introductory course in Citizenship were classified by personality types (according to their scores on the revised form of the American Council on education Inventory of Beliefs by the procedure previously described). Separate sections were organized for the "stereopaths," the "anti-authoritarians" and the "rationalists"—unbeknown of course to the students. The same teacher taught all the experimental sections, though he was not forwarned as to which group was which. The syllabus, texts, projects and schedule were kept the same. Students were tested at the beginning and the end of the term on their critical thinking ability in social science, and their social and political beliefs. They all took the same examinations. The instructor kept a weekly diary of what happened in the three sections. In the analysis of comparative accomplishments at the end, the students in the experimental sections were matched (in terms of their thinking ability) with "control" students who had not been assigned to the special sections and who did not conform to one of the three personality types. They were also compared with students of corresponding personality traits (SN and R) who were in the regular heterogeneous sections and not known to their instructors as special personality types.

It is clear that the authoritarian-type students started with a substantial handicap in comparison with the non-authoritarian and rationalists. They were far less able to "think critically" in the social science field (though not necessarily less intelligent on a non-verbal basis). They were, as a group, very poor readers. Yet in the course, the authoritarians improved their critical thinking capacity more than any of the others, though they still fell well short of the skill of their fellows. The rationalists and non-authoritarians did not significantly change their beliefs during the course; the control students showed a modest liberalization; the authoritarians made the greatest change—in the liberal direction. Because they started with such dogmatic and authoritarian stereotypes however, they did not catch up to the liberalism of the control students (whose outlook had been much more flexible and unprejudiced to begin with) and of course were still far away from the outlook of the students who started as extreme "liberals."

Perhaps the most significant finding from the standpoint of educational policy—though necessarily still tentative—was that the authoritarian students fared much better both in academic accomplishment and in liberalization of belief if they were grouped together and taught separately than if they were mixed in with other types of students. The progress made by students of this type in the experimental section was substantial, if not outstanding. Students of similar personality in the general sections made a poor record. What is more, the personal response of the students in the experimental group became more vital as the course went on. Their interest seemed to grow and they became much more active participants in the class. Excerpts from the instructor's diary reveal this gradual opening up of the authoritarian personality under patient, prolonged prodding and, be it admitted, rather "directive" teaching.

1st week—asked few questions, seemed lacking in curiosity or initiative either in reference to administrative details or discussion. More direct questioning was required to get class discussion and there was much less interplay between the students.

2nd week—continued to be reticent except in one or two cases and these proved to have gotten in class erroneously and were removed. In reading first quizzes, I discovered many of them are interested in religion.

4th week—very difficult to get discussion though direct questions indicate they are well informed on text. Constant temptation to lecture rather than discuss. One gets an attitude of "you tell us" and "we'll write on the exam."

5th week—found that with five or six times as much effort I could draw out some real discussion. Almost one half the class eventually got into the argument and there was more volunteering than previously.

7th week—discussion breakthrough to a higher level of participation— more individual cases in this class than before of willingness to fight back against the brutally dogmatic totalitarian rantings of the professor— they indignantly but politely told me I was wrong. Class was more relaxed. Just before the exam they finally broke down and asked one interpretative question after another.

8th week—group finds reliance on God or some other firm power— removes necessity of relying on others so much. Their easiest adjustment is to bear their problems without relying on other persons in academic life. Theology is easier—a formula more comfortable if you have major intellectual shortcomings.

9th week—far more cooperative, discuss more. But reticence and apparent inexperience in discussion is such that the folks need a leading question every second or third statement while with issues well developed in the 1:15 class (Rationalists) it was possible to pull out as discussion leader for about 15 minutes and watch the students fight back and forth.

10th week—discussion still moderately more difficult but everyone recited during the week, practically all *volunteering* some answers. This is a terrific contrast to the situation up to about November 7.

Special Project (involving small teams studying and reaching recommendations in regard to a local racially integrated housing program).— Slower catching on to system. I had to re-explain items. Bitter internecine warfare in their groups—came up with minority and majority reports— fought and argued with each other, uninhibited in name calling or in fanatic support for their points of view. Impression of everyone denouncing everyone else at once. Appeared that researchers had picked out and remembered the factual materials which supported their point of view. Contrary material they often neglected.

All this adds up to a conclusion of this order: The more a student is in need of direction and respects authority, the less will he respond to a course which in content or method of instruction stresses individual responsibility for value judgments and conduct. The more a student is self-reliant and resistant to authority, the more likely are his values to be affected by general education which is individualized and permissive. But the Syracuse experiment suggests that general education may be able to reach through even to the authoritarian personality, *if* it is consciously directed to his particular needs and sensitive to his problems. Much more imaginative and devoted effort than has heretofore been expended on such students is called for. This is in some ways the most challenging of the tasks now confronting general education in the social sciences.

A Note on Further Inquiry

THE results of the present exploratory study indicate the need for much more intensive research to determine accurately how students are or are not influenced by their college education, and to discover what factors do make some difference in the value-outcomes of the college experience. The findings suggested here are tentative.

LIMITATIONS OF THE EXPLORATORY STUDY

For one thing, we need more complete, more representative and more comparable data than this study has uncovered.

The meager amount of trend data, indicative of developing values over a period of years, is particularly noticeable. "Phenomenological" evidence is also lacking—for instance, personal evaluations by students or faculty of educational experiences which they believe to have influenced values. Such material would furnish greater insight into individual differences of response among students than is possible through broad surveys of attitudes and beliefs. In addition it might reveal subtle and gradual changes that are hard to spot when looking at students "en masse."

A basic shortcoming of this study is its failure to include adequate information concerning several important types of institutions, notably Roman Catholic colleges, the military academies and, with a few exceptions, southern colleges, both Negro and white. These gaps are the more significant because the influence of distinctive institutional characteristics upon student values appears so important.

The scope of the study excluded non-curricular influences. But the influence of the curriculum (at least that part of it devoted to general education) is evidently dependent on the "value-climate" of the college community which surrounds it. Instead of seeking means to isolate the curriculum as a source of impact on student values, it would probably be more profitable to try to establish the nature of the relationships which develop between a student's formal education and the rest of his college experience. In other words, we need to determine more precisely what are the circumstances in which a curriculum has "carry-over" into the student's total round of life, and in turn what is the effect of activities outside of class upon the value-outcomes of courses.

Another limitation is the lack of an adequate evaluation of the effect on student values of special types of instruction which include "laboratory practices" in social science or other projects which expose students to value-laden experiences. Many who have fashioned or participated in such programs are convinced that they have a profound influence on students. But these efforts usually have not been subjected to rigorous and objective appraisal, at least at the college level, and their actual effects on the behavior and basic attitudes of students remains a matter of conjecture.

Despite the exciting pioneer research which has been reported on student personality as a determinant of educational outcomes, knowledge is still limited on this problem. Little experimentation has so far been undertaken to see whether adaptations of the curriculum or of methods of instruction might enable a college to make a more effective contribution to the general education of certain types of students, notably those who tend to be rigid, dogmatic and "authoritarian." Consequently, judgments in this area must be considered speculative until further data are available.

In general, a systematic and definitive identification has yet to be made of educational situations in which a real influence upon student values is occurring. Information about peculiarly potent institutions or experiences has been secured "catch-as-catch-can." For the most part it is inadequate for a conclusive analysis of the factors accounting for exceptional impact, especially as the number of examples is quite limited, and the data so varied that different situations can hardly be compared.

Finally, the validity of almost every major conclusion in the purview of this study is open to challenge on the grounds that the various instruments used to detect and measure individual and group values lack sufficient sensitivity. This is a persistent complaint directed against research on values and undoubtedly more precise and discriminating techniques of examining values would raise confidence in the results. But the significance of what has been obtained with the available instruments should not be *over*-discounted, especially considering the extraordinary consistency in the outcomes of diverse projects, and the progressive refinements which have been introduced in the analysis of attitudes and personality. Inference plays an important part in reaching conclusions, however, and a considerable element of subjectivity necessarily has entered into the process of evaluation.

RESEARCH WHICH IS NOT NEEDED

On the other hand, in some areas the data already available are so adequate that there is probably no need to accumulate more, and the conclusions obtained so consistent that further programs of testing and verification seem hardly required. Further research does not appear necessary on such questions as:

The general profile of student values at the present time

The Cornell Social Science Research Center's survey appears sufficiently thorough and comprehensive to constitute a firm "baseline" from which to measure deviations that may emerge. Additional data of the survey type, at one or several institutions, are voluminous and serve to check and round out the Cornell study.

The general influence on values of education in the social sciences per se

The Cornell data seem conclusive in wiping out almost all distinctions of attitudes and beliefs between social science students and others. Little would probably be added to present knowledge by further comparative surveys of the attitudes of students in different fields, though when surveys are being conducted for other purposes it would be useful to include an identification of students' major fields of study. This would permit double checking the negative findings of the present data.

There is not much point to further before-and-after testing of the effects of specific courses or programs of study unless they embody elements or approaches which markedly distinguish them from the run of courses which have already been evaluated. This kind of testing (of which there has been a fair amount) has generally revealed few changes of significance in personal values and attitudes which could be associated with taking the course. The difficult methodological problem of establishing controls which would enable the specific influence of the course to be isolated from other factors operating upon the student can therefore be bypassed—because the evidence consistently indicates little or no accountable influence.

The influence of different methods of instruction

Research on this subject has reached a high point of refinement, and has been conducted at a variety of institutions. While the verdict is not unanimous, the evidence is strong that none of the major techniques of instruction has had such a consistently different effect on students' values from the others that it deserves a more intensive appraisal.

MAJOR PROBLEMS MERITING FURTHER STUDY

Considering the present state of research, the following problems, among others, deserve major emphasis in further inquiry:

1. How valid are the negative conclusions which have emerged regarding curricular influences on student values? For instance, would they be confirmed by a more precise and penetrating examination of *individual* student responses than was possible in the sweeping survey made here of readily accessible data concerning the reactions of a broad mass of students? Does the evidence truly reflect students' values or is there an unrecognized hiatus between what students *say* are their values and how they actually behave or would behave in situations which put their values to the test? How universally representative are the conclusions which have been drawn?

2. What factors are responsible for the unusual influence upon student values which occurs at some institutions? To what extent are these factors reproducible elsewhere?

3. What special elements in the design and conduct of programs of general education may help to break through the personality barriers which block the intellectual, social and moral growth of a large segment of the students now coming to college?

4. How significantly are the values of students influenced when first-hand experience with basic problems of human relations is deliberately made a part of their college education?

5. How can the personal influence of the college teacher be strengthened in the context of general education for the mass of students?

PROPOSALS FOR LONGER-RANGE INQUIRIES

Whether these problems can be encompassed within a single, integrated program of research is doubtful. Instead, several different types of study might profitably be undertaken—perhaps concurrently—and their end-results brought to bear in some systematic way upon the central issues. Important next steps of inquiry might include:

1. *Analysis of "phenomenological" data concerning the influence of educational experiences on students.*

a) A sampling of students at one or more institutions could be invited to prepare full open-end letters, giving a kind of life-history of their college education. They would be asked in particular what effects they felt their courses and teachers had had upon their attitudes, beliefs, vocational choices and, in general, the conduct and direction of their lives.

b) Systematic interviewing of a sample of students could be undertaken to supplement the written replies.

c) Panels of student "informants" might be useful as sounding boards to evaluate tentative findings and furnish a clearer understanding of their meaning and significance.

d) Student reports of an autobiographical nature are already available at a number of institutions (see the Inventory of Data). Some of these are worth subjecting to content-analysis.

2. *Systematic observation by teachers of the value-responses of their students.*

a) Faculty "logs" of their classroom (and out-of-class) experiences would provide a type of data almost totally lacking at present. Allowing for a subjective bias, and also for the inability of most teachers to see more than the short-run and surface responses of their students, a regularly kept diary of what goes on in a class during a semester can be a very revealing instrument.

A collection of such diaries from a well-selected cross-section of teachers in general education programs would be a counterpart to the student educational life-histories suggested above.

A broad guide noting the type of items to be included in the diaries would be helpful to the faculty preparing them, and also facilitate analysis and comparison of the experiences.

b) Small faculty round tables, lasting a week or so, would be useful to record and appraise influences of general education on student values. This project would have the special advantage of permitting teachers to compare their experiences and mutually evaluate them.

3. *Intensive studies of changes in student values at particular institutions.*

A cooperative intercollegiate study should find out just *how* and if possible *why* student values change more significantly at some institutions than others. It would be helpful if the colleges concerned could work together on a common design, so that data gathered would be as comparable as possible.

The study should be planned for at least a three-year period—the first year devoted to consultation, planning and organization; the second to active research and the collection of data on each campus; the third to analysis and evaluation. If longitudinal studies of changes in student values were included, the time devoted to the gathering of data should be extended at least another year, so as to follow an entering class through to the end of its sophomore year (this being the point at which major value changes have probably been consummated).

The research design should be eclectic, and provide for:

a) the measurement of a broad range of values of students at each main stage of their college career. Preferably such measurements should be done not only by questionnaire, but also by an activities inventory and checked by selective interviewing. With this should be coupled, of course, adequate biographical data.

b) educational life-histories by students and young alumni along the lines described above, so that the sources of their value changes could be explored subjectively.

c) analysis of the pervasiveness of certain value assumptions and goals throughout the institution. The strength and coherence of institutional norms should be assessed, and in particular the degree to which students, faculty and administration share common standards and aspirations. This probably calls for perceptive observation by both outsiders and persons having an intimate acquaintance with each campus. One can also use objective instruments to compare the priorities of values held by students with those of faculty and college officials.

d) examination of the intimacy and quality of faculty-student relationships, both in class and outside.

e) assessment of the educational and social implications for students of the institution's vital statistics, e.g., size, faculty-student ratio, library and other educational resources, administrative control and organization, advisory system, residence arrangements.

4. *Testing out experimental approaches to general education for students whose personality and upbringing have restricted their sensitivity to human values and made both their minds and their beliefs unusually inflexible.*

The pioneer experiment at Syracuse, grouping students of different personality types in special sections of the Citizenship course affords one model for this kind of inquiry. Identical instruction was provided. Outcomes were appraised both objectively and subjectively by both participants and outsiders. The "battery" of instruments included:

a) Tests of intelligence, academic subject competence and performance, and attitudes and beliefs, administered to students before and at the end of the course.

b) Student opinionnaire appraising the course and the instruction. (This might be extended to include student impressions of the effect of the course on their personal ideas and outlook).

c) Weekly diary kept by the instructor, summarizing and commenting on what transpired in class.

d) Faculty evaluations of each student's performance and response in subsequent classes.

e) Comments by dormitory counselors on each student's life and development during the year.

Enough students were taking the same course so that adequate controls could be worked out to hold constant such factors as aptitude, and the influence of particular instructors. One shortcoming was that students became aware of an ulterior motive in the way they were sectioned, though they did not know the real basis of selection.

As previously indicated, the value of much further testing of course outcomes is questionable. If done adequately, it is an elaborate and expensive operation. And in view of our findings about distinctive institutional influences a given type of course would have to be tested at a variety of institutions to permit reliable conclusions as to its general influence.

But the problem of educating the "authoritarian students" is such a critical one and so unexplored that a major pilot effort on this scale may be justified.

5. *A special study of the influence on student values of "education by experience," evaluating the outcomes of general education programs in which student action projects of different kinds have played a major role.*

Here again, an adequate methodology of appraisal is imperative if the study is worth undertaking. Neither impressionistic nor objective assessments by themselves would give the balance and depth necessary for a solid conclusion. Both types of evaluation should be used. This is particularly advisable here, because of the strong, almost doctrinaire, conviction of success held by leading protagonists of this type of education.

Inventory of the Data

(following on pages 138-174)

I. Profiles of student values
  A. General surveys of values held by students
  B. Surveys of particular attitudes or values
    1. International
    2. Politics and political participation
    3. Religious
    4. Social and political tolerance or prejudice
  C. Value studies of college graduates

II. Changes or persistence of student values
  A. Longitudinal studies
  B. Horizontal studies
  C. Secular trends

III. Curricular influences on student values
  A. Before-and-after studies of course outcomes
  B. Surveys of student and alumni opinion concerning their educational experiences
  C. Intellectual and educational autobiographies of students
  D. Analysis of distinctive value-patterns by field of study
  E. Other revelant studies

IV. The impact of the instructor
  A. Student assessments
  B. Non-student assessments.

V. Effects of teaching methods
  A. Student-centered teaching
  B. The discussion method
  C. The problems approach. Laboratory practices in social science
  D. Teaching by television
  E. Other appraisals

VI. Value-profiles of particular institutions

VII. Personality determinants of educational outcomes

VIII. Value research—methodology and instruments

IX. Selected critiques of general education and its objectives

I. PROFILES OF STUDENT VALUES

A. GENERAL SURVEYS OF VALUES HELD BY STUDENTS

American Council on Education: *The Cooperative Study in General Education;* and *The Cooperative Study of Evaluation in General Education*

These two studies, conducted from 1939–1944 and 1949–1954 respectively, collected a great variety of data on students at a wide range of institutions.

The most pertinent to the purposes of the present report were the responses to the Inventory of Beliefs and the Test of Critical Thinking in Social Science. Each of these instruments was administered (in the second of the above studies) on one or more occasions at some nineteen cooperating institutions. The tests were found to have a high degree of statistical reliability and validity. Their results are reported and analyzed in the following three references:

1. Dressel, Paul L. and Mayhew, Lewis B. *General Education: Explorations in Evaluation.* Washington, D. C.: American Council on Education, 1954.

   This is the main report of the Cooperative Study of Evaluation in General Education.

2. Manuals of instructions for the Inventory of Beliefs and other instruments used in the study. Published by the Educational Testing Service, Princeton, N. J.

3. Dressel, Paul L. and Mayhew, Lewis B. *Critical Thinking in Social Science.* Dubuque, Iowa: Wm. C. Brown Company, 1954.

   An important extension of the work done in the Cooperative Study of Evaluation was undertaken by George G. Stern, using a modified form of the Inventory of Beliefs as a means of classifying personality types. See below number 15.

   Of the original American Council Cooperative Study in General Education, the following reports contain significant material concerning the values of college students:

4. Dunkel, Harold B. *General Education in the Humanities.* Washington, D. C.: American Council on Education, 1947.

5. Levi, Albert W. *General Education in the Social Studies.* Washington, D. C.: American Council on Education, 1948.

This includes analysis of the results of inventories of students' social understanding, and beliefs about postwar reconstruction.

The Cornell Values Survey

Conducted by the Social Science Research Center of Cornell University, this has been the most comprehensive survey of the attitudes and values of American students so far undertaken. A lengthy questionnaire was first tried out at Cornell University itself in 1950 under a Carnegie Corporation grant. Then in 1952 it was administered to 4585 students representing a cross-section of the male undergraduates at 11 universities: UCLA, Cornell, Dartmouth, Fisk, Harvard, Michigan, North Carolina, Texas, Wayne, Wesleyan and Yale. Analysis of the data is still in process, but two reports have been issued, one presenting the findings concerning students' attitudes toward military service; the other dealing just with the attitudes of Cornell students. These findings have also been summarized in several articles (listed below). A volume dealing with college society as a social institution will contain the larger findings of the Cornell values study.

In addition, the Social Science Research Center generously made available to the Hazen Foundation for the purposes of this report a special tabulation of the findings, broken down by the students' field of study.

The reports on the Cornell student values survey, published to date, are:

6. Suchman, Edward A., Williams, Robin M. Jr. and Goldsen, Rose K. *Student to Soldier.* A Study of the Impact of Impending Military Service and the Present International Crisis upon College Students' Attitudes and Behavior. Cornell University: Social Science Research Center, August 1952.

7. Suchman, Edward A., Williams, Robin M. Jr. and Goldsen, Rose K. "Reactions of College Students to Manpower Policies and the Military Service Prospect," *Educational Record,* April 1953.

8. ———. "Student Reaction to Impending Military Service," *American Sociological Review,* June 1953.

9. Goldsen, Rose K. *Report on the Cornell Student Body.* Cornell University: Social Science Research Center, June 1951.

10. Blau, Peter M. "Orientation of College Students Toward International Relations," *American Journal of Sociology,* 49, 3, November 1953.

10a. Rosenberg, M. "Psychological Depression and Educational Attitudes," *Student Medicine*, October 1956.

10b. ———. "Misanthropy and Political Ideology," *American Sociological Review*, December 1956.

The Autobiography to 2000 A.D.

A cross-national study, directed by James W. Gillespie and Gordon W. Allport of Harvard University, undertook to find out how youth in various countries view the future. Students were asked to write a personal essay concerning their expectations, plans, and aspirations for the future—an "Autobiography: From Now to 2000 A.D." These were supplemented by a 50-item questionnaire. This approach provided unusual insight into a student's values, sensitive both to his individuality and the characteristics he had in common with his cultural group. The American sample was drawn from Harvard, Radcliffe and Miami. Independently, Ira DeA. Reid collected similar data at Haverford College from the entire freshman class entering in the fall of 1952.

Findings from the original study are presented in:

11. Gillespie, James M. and Allport, Gordon W. *Youth's Outlook on the Future*. New York: Random House, Inc., 1955.

12. *The Cross-Cultural Research Group*

A survey of the effects of modernization upon youth is one of the projects of an international cooperative group begun in 1952 under the sponsorship of Rice Institute, to conduct research in the behavioral sciences and now supported by a grant from the Ford Foundation. A questionnaire has been developed to ascertain student attitudes and opinions on family and social relations, religion and other questions, and is being administered to broad samples of students in the United States and Middle Eastern countries. Bradford B. Hudson and Robert B. MacLeod are the United States members of the Research Group. Two progress reports have been issued, the latest in December 1955.

Other general surveys of student values

13. Hottel, Althea K. *How Fare American Women?* A Report of the Commission on the Education of Women of the American Council on Education. Washington: American Council on Education, 1955.

14. Knode, Jay C. "Attitudes on State University Campuses," *American Sociological Review*, 8, 1943.

15. Stern, George G., Stein, Morris I. and Bloom, Benjamin S. *Methods in Personality Assessment.* Glencoe, Illinois: The Free Press, 1956. Chapter X, "A Synthetic Study of College Freshmen."

16. Todd, J. Edward. *Social Norms and the Behavior of College Students.* Teachers College Contributions to Education No. 833, 1941.

B. SURVEYS OF PARTICULAR ATTITUDES OR VALUES

International

Carnegie Endowment for International Peace. *Studies in Universities and World Affairs.*

Over 100 institutions cooperated with the Carnegie Endowment in surveying and appraising the range of their activities—curricular, extra-curricular and research—which bore on world affairs. Each college planned and conducted its own study, under the overall direction of Howard E. Wilson. Several included inquiries concerning student attitudes, and the influence of courses upon their understanding of world affairs.

The institutions' individual reports were distributed by the Endowment as mimeographed documents.

A comprehensive appraisal of the accumulated data is appearing in a series of eight volumes, as follows:

20. Baker, Vincent. *World Affairs and the College Curriculum* (in process).

21. Cole, Fred and Sterling, Richard W. *World Affairs in Institutions of Higher Education in the South* (in process).

22. Du Bois, Cora. *Foreign Students and Higher Education in the United States.* Washington: American Council on Education, 1956.

23. Fuller, C. Dale. *Training of Specialists in International Relations* (in process).

24. Gange, John. *University Research on World Affairs* (in process).

25. Houle, Cyril O. and Nelson, Charles A. *The University, the Citizen and World Affairs* (in process).

26. Wilson, Howard E. *American College Life as Education in World Outlook.* Washington: American Council on Education, 1956.

27. ———. *American University in World Affairs: A General Report* (in process).

28. World University Service. *Education for International Understanding.*

The survey included a questionnaire, answered by 7000 students at 30 institutions, concerning the extent and sources of their interest in contributing to better international understanding. Howard P. Smith of Bennington College analyzed the data and reported his findings in a report (mimeo) to World University Service, 20 W. 40th Street, New York. 1954.

29. University of Mississippi: Day, D. D. and Quackenbush, O. F. "Attitudes Toward Defensive, Cooperative and Aggressive War," *Journal of Social Psychology*, 16, 1942.

Politics and political participation ("citizenship")

30. Citizenship Education Project, Teachers College, Columbia University. *Laboratory Practices in Citizenship Education for College Students.* New York: Teachers College, Columbia University, 1955.

31. Committee of Seventy. Survey of information about politics and interest in political participation of students at Bryn Mawr College, Temple University, University of Pennsylvania and Philadelphia high schools. Summarized in *The Sunday Bulletin*, October 23, 1955, Section 2, p. 1. Original data unpublished.

32. Drucker, A. J. and Remmers, H. H. "Citizenship Attitudes of Purdue Seniors, U. S. College Graduates and High School Pupils," *Journal of Educational Psychology*, 1951.

33. Ohio Wesleyan University. The Evaluation Service. *The Development of Attitude Scales in Practical Politics.* Ohio Wesleyan University, 1955.

34. Pace, C. Robert. "What Kind of Citizens Do College Graduates Become?" *Journal of General Education*, 3, April 1949.

35. Reed, Thomas H. and Reed, Doris D. *Evaluation of Citizenship Training and Incentive in American Colleges and Universities.* New York: Citizenship Clearing House, 1950.

36. ———. *Preparing College Men and Women for Politics.* New York: Citizenship Clearing House, 1952.

37. Turner, Henry A. "They Don't Know Much," *Frontier*, December 1955.

Survey of the political knowledge and opinions of 1550 undergraduates at the University of California, Santa Barbara College.

Religious

38. Barkley, Key L. "Development of the Moral Judgment of College Students," *Character and Personality*, 10, 1942.

Conducted at Woman's College, University of North Carolina.

39. Ferguson, Leonard W. "Socio-Psychological Correlates of the Primary Attitudes Scales—I Religionism, II Humanitarianism," *Journal of Social Psychology*, 19, 1944.

40. Gilliland, A. R. "The Attitude of College Students toward God and the Church," *Journal of Social Psychology*, 11, 1940.

41. Hall, Roy M. "Religious Beliefs and Social Values of College Students," Unpublished doctoral dissertation, Syracuse University, 1950.

42. Kirkpatrick, Clifford. *Religion and Humanitarianism.* #304, Psychological Monographs. Washington: American Psychological Association, Inc., 1949.
Beliefs of University of Minnesota students, and adults in the Twin Cities area.

43. McLean, Milton D. *Inventory of Social and Religious Concepts.* American Council on Education, 1950, 1952 and 1954 printings.
A questionnaire administered at Macalester College in 1940 to about 200 students; at De Pauw to 1200 students in 1955; and at other institutions. No published report of findings.

44. Morris, Charles. *The Open Self.* New York: Prentice-Hall, 1948.
Cross-cultural analysis of dominant philosophies of life.

45. Ross, Murray G. *Religious Beliefs of Youth.* New York: Association Press, 1950.
National Council of YMCA sponsored survey of 18–29 age group, on social, political and religious questions, questionnaire supplemented by interviews. An able Foreword by Gordon Allport compares these findings with a study of religious beliefs of Harvard-Radcliffe students by Allport, Gillespie and Young.

46. Telford, C. W. "Study of Religious Attitudes," *Journal of Social Psychology*, 31, 1950.
Campus-wide survey at University of Utah.

Social and political tolerance or prejudice

50. Allport, Gordon W. *The Nature of Prejudice.* Cambridge: Addison-Wesley Press, 1954.
The definitive study of the sources, development and characteristics of prejudice. Recommendations on how to control or reduce it. Much of the data derived from experiments with students, and analysis of their attitudes.

51. ———, and Kramer, Bernard M. "Some Roots of Prejudice," *Journal of Psychology*, 22, 1946.

Measurement of prejudiced attitudes among Darthmouth and Harvard students, and analysis of factors associated with high and low prejudice.

52. Asch, Solomon E. *Social Psychology*. New York: Prentice-Hall, 1952.

Review of studies of ethnic prejudice and tolerance. General analysis of factors affecting attitude formation. (pp. 525ff, 600ff.)

53. Cook, Lloyd and Cook, Elaine. *Intergroup Education*. New York: McGraw-Hill, 1954.

Report of the College Study on Intergroup Relations, a nation-wide four year survey including experimental projects.

54. Fay, Paul J. and Middleton, Warren C. "Factors Related to Liberal-Conservative Attitudes of College Students," *Journal of Social Psychology*, 12, 1940. (At De Pauw University).

55. Hyman, Herbert and Sheatsley, Paul. "Trends in Public Opinion on Civil Liberties," *Journal of Social Issues*, 9, 1953.

Summary of data from national polls.

56. Kerr, W. A. "Correlates of Politico-Economic Liberalism-Conservatism," *Journal of Social Psychology*, 20, 1944.

Survey of main experimental research on student liberalism.

57. Nelson, Erland. *Radicalism-Conservatism in Student Attitudes*. #224, Psychological Monographs. Columbus, Ohio: Ohio State University for American Psychological Association, Inc., 1938.

58. Samelson, Babette. "Does Education Diminish Prejudice?" *Journal of Social Issues*, 1, 1945.

59. Stemper, Herbert. "Student Opinion on Issues of Academic Freedom," *Journal of Social Issues*, 1953. (At University of California and Columbia University).

60. Stouffer, Samuel A. *Communism, Conformity and Civil Liberties*. Garden City: Doubleday, 1955.

The definitive study made for the Fund for the Republic of public opinion on civil liberties in the United States.

C. VALUE STUDIES OF COLLEGE GRADUATES

61. Havemann, Ernest and West, Patricia Salter. They Went to College: *The College Graduate in America Today*. New York: Harcourt, Brace & Co., 1952.

     Report of survey of opinions and activities of college graduates, conducted by TIME in 1947.

62.   Macalester College: alumni opinion survey in process.

(34) Pace, C. Robert. "What Kind of Citizens Do College Graduates Become?"
     Based on findings of the TIME survey.

63.   *St. Scholastica, The First Fifteen Years of the College of: A Report on the Effectiveness of Catholic Education for Women.* New York: Declan McMullen Co., 1947.
     Based on poll of alumnae.

64.   *St. Scholastika, A Second Look at the College of.* Duluth: College of St. Scholastica, 1955.

65.   Wallace, Donald G. "A Description and Interpretation of the Activities and Opinions of Syracuse Graduates Related to General Education," Unpublished doctoral dissertation, Syracuse University, 1949.

II. CHANGES OR PERSISTENCE OF STUDENT VALUES

These "trend data" provide evidence of the evolution of students' attitudes, beliefs and conduct during their college careers, and in a few cases of what happens to their values after graduation.

A.   LONGITUDINAL STUDIES: examining the attitudes of the same individuals over a period of time. These concern broad developments related to the students' college experience as a whole rather than changes occurring in a specific course. Studies of the latter type are listed later.

70.   Antioch College: Studies by the Office of Testing and Evaluation based on ACE Inventory of Beliefs and Critical Thinking Test administered to freshmen, November 1951, and retaken in March 1952 by the same students.

71.   Arsenian, Seth. "Changes in Evaluative Attitude," *Journal of Applied Psychology,* 27, 1943.
     A thorough inquiry into the values of students at Springfield College conducted over a full college generation, using Allport-Vernon Study of Values, supplemented by interviews.

(38) Barkley, Key L. "Development of the Moral Judgment of College Students."

72.   Bender, Irving. Study of value changes over twenty years among Dartmouth College graduates (in process, 1955–1956).

Retake of the Allport-Vernon study of values on original subjects.

73. Bugelski, Richard and Lester, Olive. "Changes in Attitudes of College Students during their College Course and After Graduation," *Journal of Social Psychology*, 12, 1940.
Conducted at University of Buffalo.

74. Carlin, Edward, Nosow, Sigmund, and others. Study of outcomes of the introductory social science course in the Basic College, Michigan State University.
ACE Inventory of Beliefs and Critical Thinking in Social Science Test given to entire freshman class on entrance in 1954; repeated with those completing introductory social science course in spring of 1955. Biographical data for all students. Interviews with random sample to secure personal reactions to course.

(280) Churchill, Ruth. "Evaluation of General Education at Antioch College."

75. Colgate University: ACE Inventory of Beliefs and other tests administered to freshmen at entrance; readministered at end of sophomore year.

76. Corey, Stephen M. "Changes in Opinions of Female Students after one year at a University," *Journal of Social Psychology*, 11, 1940.
Conducted at the University of Wisconsin.

(1) Dressel, Paul L. and Mayhew, Lewis B. *General Education: Explorations in Evaluation*. Chapters 7 and 8.

77. Farnsworth, Paul R. "Changes in Attitude Toward War During College Years," *Journal of Social Psychology*, 8, 1937.
Conducted at Stanford University.

(9) Goldsen, Rose K. *Report on the Cornell Student Body*.

78. Hunter, E. C. "Changes in Attitudes of Women Students During Four Years in College," *Journal of Social Psychology*, 16, 1942.
Conducted at Converse College.

79. Jones, V. A. "Attitudes of College Students and Changes in Such Attitudes during Four Years in College," *Journal of Educational Psychology*, 29, 1938.
Conducted at Clark University.

80. Kelly, E. Lowell. "Consistency of the Adult Personality," *American Psychologist*, 10, 11, November 1955.

81. Kuhlen, Raymond G. "Changes in Attitudes of Students," *School & Society*, 53, 1941.
Conducted at Ohio State University.

82. McCann, Richard V. "Developmental Factors in the Growth of a Mature Faith," *Religious Education*, May-June, 1955.
   Based on intimate interviews with a sample of adults.

83. Nelson, Erland N. P. *Persistence of Attitudes of College Students 14 Years Later.* #373, Psychological Monographs. Washington: American Psychological Association, Inc., 1954.

84. Newcomb, Theodore M. "The Influence of Attitude Climates upon Some Determinants of Information," *Journal of Abnormal and Social Psychology*, 41, 1946.
   Comparison of changes in student attitudes at Bennington College, Catholic University of America, and Williams College.

85. ———. *Personality and Social Change: Attitude Formation in a Student Community.* New York: Dryden Press, 1943.
   An intensive analysis of attitude changes at Bennington College, 1935–1939.

(111) Pace, C. Robert. "Liberalism and Knowledge of Current Affairs."

87. Princeton University: Intensive study of attitudes and responses of sample of undergraduates throughout their college career. Discussions recorded confidentially of periodic preceptorial conferences, with opportunity for students' discussion of all matters of concern to them. Analysis in a preliminary stage, 1955–1956.

88. Sarah Lawrence College: Intensive analysis of the development of student personality, attitudes and emotional adjustment during the college career. Detailed evaluations of students by faculty and psychological consultant; comprehensive testing program, including Minnesota Multiphasic, Rorschach; personal statements by students at entrance and periodically through college, concerning their educational objectives, interests and beliefs. Overall appraisal in preparation (1956) by Lois Murphy, Irving Goldman, Harold Taylor and others.

(147) Syracuse University: ACE test of Critical Thinking in Social Science and Inventory of Beliefs administered on admission and later as end-tests.

(16) Todd, J. Edward. *Social Norms and the Behavior of College Students.*

89. Vassar College: "Mellon Project": Comprehensive evaluation of impact of Vassar on its students, supported by the Mellon Foundation. Battery of tests given to entering freshmen and again administered in senior year. Program for interviewing a random sample of one class from time to time throughout their college courses. Testing and Assessment of Alumnae. Pres-

ent analysis of changes for one college generation have led to the construction of the "Vassar developmental scale," an index of the characteristics in which seniors are markedly different from freshmen. Directed by Nevitt Sanford.

90. Wallace, Donald G. "Evaluation Practices in General Education at Drake University," chapter XI in Dressel, Paul L. *Evaluation in General Education* (200).

91. Whitely, Paul L. "The Constancy of Personal Values," *Journal of Abnormal and Social Psychology*, 33, 1938.

Allport-Vernon Study of Values administered to students at Franklin and Marshall College each year throughout college.

B. HORIZONTAL STUDIES: Comparing the attitudes at a given time of students who are at different stages of college

(51) Allport, Gordon W. and Kramer, Bernard M. "Some Roots of Prejudice."

(282) Antioch College. *Report to the Rockefeller Foundation.*

100. Boldt, J. W. and Stroud, J. B. "Changes in the Attitudes of College Students," *Journal of Educational Psychology*, 25, 1934.

Survey at Kansas State Teachers College, Emporia.

101. Burgemeister, B. B. "The Permanence of Interests of Women College Students," *Arch. Psych.* 255, 1940.

102. Cantey, Evelyn and Mull, Helen. "A Comparison of Freshmen and Seniors in. . . . Understanding of Social Issues," *Journal of Social Psychology*, 16, 1942. (At Sweet Briar College.)

103. Cantril, H. and Allport, Gordon W. "Recent Applications of the Study of Values," *Journal of Abnormal and Social Psychology*, 28, 1933.

Summary and analysis of early results of Allport-Vernon Study of Values.

(53) Cook, Lloyd and Cook, Elaine. *Intergroup Education.*

(6–10) Cornell University Social Science Research Center. *Survey of Student Values.*

(191–194) Downie, N. M., Pace, C. R. and Troyer, M. E. Opinions of Syracuse University students.

(32) Drucker, A. J. and Remmers, H. H. "Citizenship Attitudes of Purdue Seniors."

105. Dukes, William. "Psychological Studies of Values," *Psychological Bulletins*, January 1955.

A good summary of psychological research in field of values.

(4)   Dunkel, Harold B. *General Education in the Humanities.*

106.   Emme, Earle E. "Changes in Student Attitudes," *Phi Delta Kappan*, 26, 1943.
Summary of research studies.

107.   Fischer, Robert P. and Andrews, Avonne L. "Effect of Conformity to Social Expectancy on Evaluative Attitudes," *Educational and Psychological Measurement*, 17, 1947.

(40)   Gilliland, A. R. "The Attitude of College Students Toward God and Church."

108.   Havighurst, Robert J. "Moral Character and Religious Education," *Religious Education*, 51, 3, May–June 1956.

(41)   Hall, Roy M. "Religious Beliefs and Social Values of College Students."

(55)   Hyman, Herbert and Sheatsley, Paul. "Trends in Public Opinion on Civil Liberties."

109.   Katz, Daniel and Allport, Floyd H. *Students' Attitudes.* Syracuse, New York: Craftsman Press, 1931.
An outstanding early opinion study, conducted at Syracuse University.

(56)   Kerr, W. A. "Correlates of Politico-Economic Liberalism-Conservatism."

(5)   Levi, Albert. *General Education in the Social Studies.* Reports variations in attitudes of freshmen and other classes on Inventory of Social Understanding and Inventory of Beliefs About Postwar Reconstruction. Also pre- and post-tests, 86 ff.

110.   Marcuse, F. L. "Attitudes and Their Relationships," *Journal of Abnormal and Social Psychology*, 40, 1945.
An experiment with a small class in industrial relations at Cornell University.

(287)   Michigan State University: Board of Examiners. Tests, including ACE Inventory of Beliefs, administered to freshmen and samples of upperclassmen, 1951–1952.

(57)   Nelson, Erland. *Radicalism-Conservatism in Student Attitudes.*

(33)   Ohio Wesleyan University. The Evaluation Service. *The Development of Attitude Scales in Practical Politics.*

111.   Pace, C. Robert. "Liberalism and Knowledge of Current Affairs," *Journal of Social Psychology*, 10, 1939.

112.   ———. "University-Wide Studies in Evaluation of General Education at Syracuse University," in Dressel, Paul L. *Evaluation in General Education* (200).

(34) ———. "What Kind of Citizens Do College Graduates Become?"

113. Schaefer, Benjamin R. "The Validity and Utility of the Allport-Vernon Study of Values Test," *Journal of Abnormal and Social Psychology*, 30, 1936.

114. Southwestern at Memphis. *The Study of Values; Final Report.*
Allport-Vernon Study of Values administered to all students, 1952–1953, also to faculty, sample of alumni and 200 liberal arts graduates of a state university.

115. Spoerl, Dorothy. "Some Aspects of Prejudice as Affected by Religion and Education," *Journal of Social Psychology*, 33, 1951.

116. Wesleyan University: Special analysis of differences between freshmen and other classes in responses to Cornell Values survey.

C. SECULAR TRENDS IN STUDENT ATTITUDES

117. Breemes, E. L., Remmers, H. H. and Morgan, C. L. "Changes in Liberalism-Conservatism of College Students Since the Depression," *Journal of Social Psychology*, 14, 1941.

118. Pressey, S. L. "Changes from 1923 to 1943 in the Attitudes of Public School and University Students," *Journal of Psychology*, 21, 1946.

III. CURRICULAR INFLUENCES ON STUDENT VALUES

A. BEFORE-AND-AFTER STUDIES; measuring changes in beliefs and attitudes during particular courses or programs. Those studies which have undertaken specific analyses of the influence of different teachers or methods of instruction are listed separately in later sections

120. Antioch College: Office of Testing and Evaluation. Analysis of impact of general education courses in History and American Government on scores made by students on ACE Inventory of Beliefs.

121. Billings, Elizabeth L. "The Influence of a Social Studies Experiment on Student Attitudes," *School & Society*, 56, 1942. (Colby Junior College).

122. Bloom, Benjamin S. "Changing Conceptions of Examining at

the University of Chicago," in Dressel, Paul L. *Evaluation in General Education*. (200).

(74) Carlin, Edward, Nosow, Sigmund and others. Study of outcomes of social science course in the Basic College, Michigan State University.

(53) Cook, Lloyd and Cook, Elaine. *Intergroup Education*.

123. Eckert, Ruth E. *Outcomes of General Education*. Minneapolis: University of Minnesota Press, 1943. p. 96; chap. 10.
Appraisal of the program of the General College, University of Minnesota.

124. Fersh, George L. "Changes in Social Beliefs and Social Values Effected by a Social Studies Course Based on the Problems Approach," Unpublished doctoral dissertation, New York University, 1949. (At New York University, School of Education).

125. Gerberich, J. R. and Jamison, A. W. "Measurement of Attitudinal Changes during an Introductory Course in Sociology," *Journal of Educational Psychology*, 8, 1934. (At University of Arkansas).

126. Harvard University: Value changes during a course in Human Relations (Bales' Value Profile administered before and after taking course).

127. Haverford College: Social Science Staff. Study of impact of introductory social science course on political attitudes (Stouffer test administered before and after first segment of the course)—in process 1955–1956.

128. Hovland, Carl I., Janis, Irving L. and Kelley, Harold H. *Communication and Persuasion*; Psychological Studies of Opinion Changes. New Haven: Yale University Press, 1953.

129. Jones, O. Garfield. "Is Civic Education a Fraud?" *National Municipal Review*, May 1952.
Results of "effective citizenship" course at University of Toledo.

130. Kelley, Harold and Pepitone, Albert. "An Evaluation of a College Course in Human Relations," *Journal of Educational Psychology*, 43, April 1952. (At Massachusetts Institute of Technology).

131. Kornhauser, Arthur W. "Changes in Information and Attitudes of Students in an Economics Course," *Journal of Educational Research*, 22, 1930. (At University of Chicago).

132. McQuitty, John V. "Evaluation in General Education at the University of Florida," Chap. VIII in Dressel, Paul L. *Evaluation in General Education* (200).

133. Morris, John B. "Critical Thinking Gains and Achievement in a Social Science Course," Unpublished doctoral dissertation, Syracuse University, 1953. (At Syracuse University).

134. Muelder, Hermann R. "An Interdepartmental Course for Seniors," *Journal of Higher Education, 25, February* 1954. (At Knox College).

135. New York University, Washington Square College of Liberal Arts: Analysis of impact of general course in social science on student political interest and attitudes; compared with regular course in American government. See Somit *et al* (145) for progress report.

(33) Ohio Wesleyan University. The Evaluation Service. *The Development of Attitude Scales in Practical Politics.*

136. ———: Pre- and post-tests of attitudes in an integrated introductory course in social science and in an introductory course in philosophy.

(111) Pace, C. Robert. "Liberalism and Knowledge of Current Affairs."

137. Pennsylvania State University: *Progress Report to Provost of the Instructional Committee of International Understanding 300*, 1956. Confidential.

137a ———: Report to the President by the University International Understanding Committee for the year 1955–1956. Mimeographed.

138. Pike, Carroll M. Jr. "A Study of the Relationship of Selected Socio-Economic Factors to Outcomes of the Program of General Education at Michigan State College," Unpublished Ed. D. dissertation, Michigan State University, 1953.

139. Reed College: Jones, Richard and others. Evaluations of Senior "integrating" seminar established under Carnegie Corporation grant (in process, 1955–1956).

(35) Reed, Thomas H. and Reed, Doris D. *Evaluation of Citizenship Training and Incentive in American Colleges and Universities.*

(36) ———. *Preparing College Men and Women for Politics.*

140. Salner, E. and Remmers, H. H. "Affective Selectivity and Liberalizing Influences of College Course," *Journal of Applied Psychology*, 17, 1933. (At Purdue University).

141. Schonbar, Rosalea Ann. "Student Attitudes Toward Communists: The Relation Between Intensity of Attitude and Amount of Information," *Journal of Psychology*, 27, 1949. (At Wheaton College, Illinois).

142. Smith, George H. "Liberalism and Level of Information," *Journal of Educational Psychology*, 1948.

143. Smith, Henry C. and Dunbar, Donald. "Personality and Achievement of Classroom Participant," *Journal of Educational Psychology*, 1951.

144. Smith, Mapheus. "Spontaneous Change of Attitude Toward War," *School & Society*, 46, 1937. (At University of Kansas).

145. Somit, Albert, Nealon, Rita W. and Wilke, Walter H. "Evaluating the Effects of Social-Science Instruction," *Journal of Higher Education*, 26, 6, June 1955.

Political participation and attitudes inquiries given before and after general course in social science at Washington Square College of Liberal Arts, New York University, and to control groups taking other introductory social science courses at the same institution (in process, 1953–1956).

146. Stern, George G. and Cope, Alfred H. "Differences in educability between stereopaths, non-stereopaths, and rationals," *American Psychologist*, 11, 8, 1956.

Experimental study of effects of personality or prior patterns of belief on educational accomplishment in citizenship course at Syracuse University. Students with similar scores on Inventory of Beliefs were grouped together in experimental sections.

147. Syracuse University: ACE test of Critical Thinking in Social Science and Inventory of Beliefs administered to students on admission, retaken later by various groups as end-test.

148. Stevens, C. D. "Analysis for a Social Science Class," chapter VIII, in Levi, Albert W. *General Education in the Social Studies* (5).

(90) Wallace, Donald G. "Evaluation Practices in General Education at Drake University."

149. Whistler, Lawrence. "Changes in Attitudes toward Social Issues Accompanying a One-Year Freshman Social Science Course," *Journal of Psychology*, 10, 1940.

150. Ylvisaker, Hedvig and Pace, C. Robert. "Differential Changes in College Students' Information and attitudes in Social Studies Courses," *Social Education*, February 1940. (At University of Minnesota, General College).

151. Young, Donald. "Some Effects of a Course in American Race Problems on the Race Prejudice of 450 Undergraduates at the University of Pennsylvania," *Journal of Abnormal and Social Psychology*, 22, 1927.

B. Surveys of Student and Alumni Opinion Concerning Educational Experiences They Consider Important

159.   Antioch College: *The Antioch Graduate—A Study of His Career Planning and Later Work Adjustment.* Unpublished report.

(283)   Beloit College: *Liberal Education at Beloit College.*

(285)   Bradbury, William. *Education and Other Aspects of Personal Growth in the College Community.*

(211)   Brodbeck, Arthur J. *The Student Looks at Controversial Issues in the High School.*

160.   Carnegie Endowment for International Peace. *Universities and World Affairs.* Mimeographed papers. Document No. 37: Report on the Teaching of International Relations at Sweet Briar College.

161.   Document No. 39: A World Affairs Survey of the Pennsylvania State University.

162.   Document No. 73: State University of New York College for Teachers at Buffalo and World Affairs.

163.   Document No. 80: The State University of Iowa and World Affairs.

164.   Collins, Robert and Hammond, R. "Study of Student Attitudes Toward Education," Senior report at Haverford College, made to Prof. Ira De A. Reid. Unpublished manuscript.

165.   Cooke, Lawrence S. "An Analysis of Certain Factors Which Affect Student Attitudes Toward a Basic College Course, Effective Living," Unpublished Ed. D. dissertation, Michigan State University, 1952.

(6–   Cornell University. Social Science Research Center. *Survey of*
10)   *Student Values.*

(194)   Downie, N. M., Pace, C. R., and Troyer, M. E. "A Study of General Education at Syracuse University with Special Attention to the Objectives."

166.   Eckert, Ruth E. "Evaluation in General Education," chap. 12 in Henry, Nelson B. (ed.) *The Fifty-First Yearbook of the National Society for the Study of Education.* Part I: General Education. Chicago: University of Chicago Press, 1952.

(123)   ———. *Outcomes of General Education.*

167.   Farnsworth, Dana, Funkenstein, Daniel H. and Wedge, Bryant. "The Social and Emotional Adjustment of 'Early Admission' College Students." Draft report prepared for the Fund for the Advancement of Education. Unpublished manuscript.

(9)   Goldsen, Rose K. *Report on the Cornell Student Body.*

168. Harvard Student Council. *An Analysis of General Education at Harvard.* February 1952.

(61) Havemann, Ernest and West, Patricia Salter. *They went To College: The College Graduate in America Today.*

(78) Hunter, E. C. "Changes in Attitudes of Women Students During Four Years in College."

(109) Katz, Daniel and Allport, Floyd H. *Students' Attitudes.*

169. Litterick, William S. "Evaluation at Stephens College," chap. VI in Dressel, Paul L. *Evaluation in General Education* (200).

(62) Macalester College: Alumni opinion survey (in process).

170. Nelson, Erland. "Student Attitudes Toward the College Now Attended," *School & Society,* 48, 1938.

171. New York University: *Memorandum* to the Washington Square College Faculty from the Directing Committee of the New General Program.
     Review of concepts of general education, and a special memorandum #3 reporting student evaluation of the "new" general education program and of the "present" general education program, e.g. core courses which have been in operation several years but are less integrated than the "new" ones.

(112) Pace, C. Robert. "University-Wide Studies in Evaluation of General Education at Syracuse University."

172. Pearson, Richard. "The Students' View of Early Admission: An Evaluation of the Experiment through Essays written by 1951 Early Admission Scholars and Comparison Students." Draft Report prepared by the Educational Testing Service for the Fund for the Advancement of Education. Unpublished manuscript.

(63) *St. Scholastica, The First Fifteen Years of the College of: A Report on the Effectiveness of Catholic Education for Women.*

(64) ———, *A Second Look. . . . at the College of.*

173. San Francisco State College, Office of Curriculum Evaluation. *Evaluation Report #2: Student Opinion about General Education Courses and Faculty.* Mimeographed paper, 1953.

(291) Syracuse University. *Self-Survey,* 1949.

174. Smith, Alden W. *Participation in Organizations: A Study of Columbia College Alumni.* Teachers College Contributions to Education No. 935, 1938.

(65, 90) Wallace, Donald G. "A Description and Interpretation of the Activities and Opinions of Syracuse Graduates Related to General Education," and "Evaluation Practices in General Education at Drake University."

175. Warrington, Willard G., Kidd, John W. and Dahnke, Harold.

"General Education—Its Importance During the First Two Years of College," *Junior College Journal*, December 1955.

Student evaluation of the Basic College program at Michigan State University.

(28) World University Service: *Education for International Understanding*.

C. INTELLECTUAL AND EDUCATIONAL AUTOBIOGRAPHIES OF STUDENTS

180. Antioch College: Senior essays and freshman papers.

181. Columbia University: "Sophomore reports."

182. Cornell University: Interview data gathered by the Cornell Social Science Research Center, 1950 and 1952.

183. Fund for the Advancement of Education: "Early admission" scholarship applications.

(11) Harvard University-Radcliffe College-Miami University: *Auto-Biography: From Now to 2000 A.D.*

Essays collected from a sample of 481 male and 97 female undergraduates for a study by James M. Gillespie and Gordon W. Allport *Youth's Outlook on the Future*.

184. Haverford College: *Autobiography: From Now to 2000 A.D.*

Collected from the entering freshman class in 1952.

(87) Princeton University: Preceptorial discussions.

(88) Sarah Lawrence College: Autobiographical essays of freshmen; periodic student reports and self-appraisals.

185. Social Science Research Council. Undergraduate research stipend applications—statements concerning sources and growth of interest in social science.

(89) Vassar College: Interview data gathered in the "Mellon project."

186. Woodrow Wilson Fellowship Program: Applicants' statements concerning sources and growth of their intellectual interests.

D. ANALYSES OF DISTINCTIVE VALUE-PATTERNS BY FIELD OF STUDY

(51) Allport, Gordon W. and Kramer, Bernard M. "Some Roots of Prejudice."

(38) Barkley, Key L. "Development of the Moral Judgment of College Students."

College Students."

(100) Boldt, J. W. and Stroud, J. B. "Changes in the Attitudes of College Students."

(163) Carnegie Endowment for International Peace. *Universities and World Affairs*. Mimeographed paper. Document No. 80: The State University of Iowa and World Affairs.

(6– Cornell University Social Science Research Center. *Survey of*

10)   *Student Values.*
         Analysis of fields of study as determining factor in value
         formation, made by P. E. Jacob for Hazen Foundation on
         basis of Cornell survey data.

191.   Downie, N. M., Troyer, M. E. and Pace, C. R. "The Knowledge
         of General Education of a Sample of Syracuse University
         Students as Revealed by the Cooperative General Culture Test
         and the Time Magazine Current Affairs Test," *Educational
         and Psychological Measurement*, 10, 2, Summer 1950.

192.   ———. "The Opinions of Syracuse University Students on Some
         Widely Discussed Current Issues," *Educational and Psycho-
         logical Measurement*, 10, 4, Winter 1950.

193.   ———. "Problems in General Education Suggested by a Study
         of the Achievement and the Opinions of Syracuse University
         Students," *Educational and Psychological Measurement*, 11,
         1, Spring 1951.

194.   ———. "A Study of General Education at Syracuse University
         with Special Attention to the Objectives," *Educational and
         Psychological Measurement*, 10, 3, Autumn 1950.

(105)   Dukes, William. "Psychological Studies of Values."

(39)   Ferguson, Leonard W. "Socio-Psychological Correlates of the
         Primary Attitude Scales–I Religionism, II Humanitarianism."

(79)   Jones, V. A. "Attitudes of College Students and Changes in
         Such Attitudes during Four Years in College."

(56)   Kerr, W. A. "Correlates of Politico-Economic Liberalism-Con-
         servatism."

195.   Knapp, Robert H. and Greenbaum, Joseph J. *The Younger
         American Scholar: His Collegiate Origins.* Chicago and Middle-
         town: University of Chicago Press, 1953.
         Includes analysis of background and characteristics of
         scholars in different fields of study.

(85)   Newcomb, Theodore M. *Personality and Social Change: Attitude
         Formation in a Student Community.*

196.   Sternberg, Carl. *Personality Trait Patterns of College Students
         Majoring in Different Fields.* #403, Psychological Monographs.
         Washington: American Psychological Association, Inc., 1955.

(16)   Todd, J. Edward. *Social Norms and the Behavior of College
         Students.*

E.   OTHER RELEVANT STUDIES

198.   Columbia University. Committee on Plans (Carman, Harry J.,
         chairman). *A College Program in Action. A Review of Work-*

ing Principles at Columbia College. New York: Columbia University Press, 1946.

199. Derbigny, Irving A. *General Education in the Negro College.* Stanford University, California: Stanford University Press, 1947.

200. Dressel, Paul L. *Evaluation in General Education.* Dubuque, Iowa: Wm. C. Brown Co., 1954.

(1) ————, and Mayhew, Lewis B. *General Education: Explorations in Evaluation.*

201. Edgar, Earl E. "Values, Social Science and General Education," *Journal of General Education,* 5, April 1951.

202. Hamilton, Thomas and Blackman, Edward. *The Basic College of Michigan State.* East Lansing, Michigan: Michigan State College Press, 1955.

203. Ostlund, Leonard A. "An Evaluation of a General Education Program." *School & Society,* 81, January 8, 1955.

USAFI General Education Development tests administered to sample at Oklahoma Agricultural and Mechanical College, and high and low scorers factor analyzed. Vocationalism apparently a rigid factor accounting for low performance on General Education Development tests, as well as generally low scholarship.

204. Pace, C. Robert. "Evaluating the Outcomes of General Education," *Journal of General Education,* 1, January 1947.

205. Smith, George H. "Opinions Related to College Expectations," *Journal of Social Psychology,* 32, 1950.

IV. THE IMPACT OF THE INSTRUCTOR

A. STUDENT ASSESSMENTS: Reports on student ratings of faculty and the other data listed below provide evidence of what students think about their teachers and the factors which inspire student esteem.

210. Antioch College. Office of Testing and Evaluation. Student ratings of faculty.

(283) Beloit College. *Liberal Education at Beloit College.*

211. Brodbeck, Arthur J. *The Student Looks at Controversial Issues in the High School.* Mimeographed paper, no date.

Report on survey of college students in California and Eastern institutions, *re* their recollection of the teaching of controversial issues and other experiences in Senior High School.

A good example of a phenomenological study applied to high school, revealing also comparative evaluations of high school as against college teaching.

(74)   Carlin, Edward, Nosow, Sigmund and others. Study of outcomes of the introductory social science course in the Basic College, Michigan State University.

Includes interviews with randomly selected sample of students, appraising their instruction.

(20–26)   Carnegie Endowment for International Peace. *Studies in Universities and World Affairs.*

Included a survey of 2000 students with a query relating to the influence of faculty and other factors on students' understanding of and interest in world affairs.

212.   Coffman, William E., "Determining Students' Concepts of Effective Teaching from their Ratings of Instructors," *Journal of Educational Psychology*, 1954.

Study conducted at Oklahoma Agricultural and Mechanical College.

(165)   Cooke, Lawrence S. "An Analysis of Certain Factors which Affect Students' Attitudes toward a Basic College Course."

(200)   Dressel, Paul L. *Evaluation in General Education.*

See particularly articles on evaluation of programs at University of Florida, Michigan State University, San Francisco State College and Syracuse University.

213.   Drucker, A. J. and Remmers, H. H. "Do Alumni and Students Differ in their Attitudes Toward Instructors?" *Journal of Educational Psychology*, 1951.

Survey conducted at Purdue University.

214.   Eckert, Ruth E. and Keller, Robert J. (eds.). *A University Looks at its Program.* Minneapolis: University of Minnesota Press, 1954.

Chap. 23: Student Ratings of College Teachers. Summarizes the results of student evaluations of teaching at the University of Minnesota.

215.   Friedson, Eliot (ed.). *Student Government, Student Leaders and the American College.* Philadelphia: U. S. National Student Association, 1955.

A study of student participation in college policy-making, based on a general questionnaire and intensive interviewing of student leaders and college officials. Includes an evaluation of faculty relationship to student government and the student body (pp. 48–51).

216.   Goodhartz, Abraham S. "Student Attitudes and Opinions Relat-

ing to Teaching at Brooklyn College," *School & Society*, 68, 1948.

217. Guthrie, E. R. *The Evaluation of Teaching: A Progress Report.* Seattle: University of Washington, 1954.

    Examination of the operation and results of student ratings of faculty as conducted at the University of Washington over a period of thirty years.

218. Hart, Frank W. *Teachers and Teaching by Ten Thousand High School Seniors.* New York: Macmillan, 1934.

(168) Harvard Student Council. *An Analysis of General Education at Harvard.*

219. Hudelson, Earl. "Validity of Student Rating of Instructors," *School & Society*, 73, 1951. (At West Virginia University).

220. Krueger, Levi. "Traits in College Teachers Preferred by Students," *Phi Delta Kappan*, September 1936.

221. Mueller, F. F. "Trends in Student Rating of Faculty," *American Association of University Professors Bulletin*, 37, 1951.

222. Riley, John W., Ryan, Bryce F. and Lifshitz, Marcia. *The Student Looks at His Teacher;* an inquiry into the implications of student ratings at the college level. New Brunswick: Rutgers University Press, 1950.

    Report on the comprehensive survey conducted at Brooklyn College.

(173) San Francisco State College Office of Curriculum Evaluation. *Evaluation Report #2: Student Opinion about General Education Courses and Faculty.*

223. ———. *Evaluation Report #11: An Experiment with a Student Questionnaire on a General Education Course: Humanities 30–31.* Mimeographed paper, 1953.

(291) Syracuse University. *Self-Survey.*

    Included a student evaluation of course instruction and qualifications of outstanding teachers.

224. Taylor, B. L. "What 1,062 College Upperclassmen Thought of the Social Studies," *School & Society*, 73, 1951.

225. Voeks, Virginia. "Ridicule and Other Detriments to Effective Teaching," *American Association of University Professors Bulletin*, 40, Winter 1954–1955.

    Based on an evaluation of student ratings of faculty at the University of Washington.

(175) Warrington, Willard G., Kidd, John W. and Dahnke, Harold. "General Education—Its Importance During the First Two Years of College."

226. Wilson, Robert N. "The Undergraduate Social Scientist," *Social*

Science Research Council Items, September 1954.

Analysis of statements made by applicants for the SSRC undergraduate research stipends, concerning the sources of their interest in social science.

(186)   Woodrow Wilson Fellowship Program. Applicants' statements concerning sources and growth of their intellectual interests.

(28)   World University Service. *Study of Education for International Understanding.*

Questionnaire answered by 7000 students at 30 institutions included query relating to influence of faculty and other factors on their understanding of and interest in world affairs.

B.   Non-Student Assessments of the Influence of Teachers

230.   Axelrod, Joseph. "The Evaluation of the General Education Program at San Francisco State College," Chap. V in Dressel, Paul L. *Evaluation in General Education.* (200).

231.   Espy, R. H. Edwin. *The Religion of College Teachers.* The Beliefs, Practices and Religious Preparation of Faculty Members in Church-Related Colleges. New York: Association Press, 1951.

232.   House, R. B. "Some College Values are Caught and Not Taught," *Journal of General Education,* 2, 1948.

233.   Kershner, F. D. Jr. "Career Problems of Instructors in General Education," Unpublished manuscript.

234.   Morse, H. T. "Social Studies Teachers for College Programs of General Education," *National Council for the Social Studies Yearbook,* 1952.

235.   ————. and Cooper, Russell M. "Problems of Implementing Programs of General Education," in Morse, H. T. (ed.) *General Education in Transition: A Look Ahead.* Minneapolis: University of Minnesota Press, 1951.

236.   Naftalin, Arthur E., Hawley, Claude E. and Nelson, Benjamin. "The Social Sciences," in Morse, H. T. (ed.) *General Education in Transition: A Look Ahead,* op. cit. (235).

237.   San Francisco State College. Office of Curriculum Evaluation. *Evaluation Report #9: An Analysis of General Education Course Staffs as Cooperatively Working "Groups."* Mimeographed paper, 1953.

237a   San Francisco State College. Office of Curriculum Evaluation. *Evaluation Report #12: An Analysis of General Education Course Staff "Stability."* Mimeographed paper, 1953.

238. Sibley, Elbridge. "Education of Social Science Teachers," *Journal of General Education,* January 1949.

239. Tead, Ordway. *Character Building and Higher Education.* New York: Macmillan, 1953.

240. Williams, Cornelia D., Eckert, Ruth E. and Potthoff, Edward F. "Basic Considerations in Planning Research in General Education," in Morse, H. T. (ed.), *General Education in Transition: A Look Ahead,* op. cit. (235). Section dealing with staffing of courses.

V. EFFECTS OF TEACHING METHODS

A. STUDENT-CENTERED TEACHING

241. Asch, Morton J. *Non-directive Teaching in Psychology.* #321, Psychological Monographs. Washington: American Psychological Association, Inc., 1951.
    Experiment conducted at Mohawk College.

242. Bills, Robert E. "An Investigation of Student-Centered Teaching," *Journal of Educational Research,* 46, 1952.
    Conducted at University of Kentucky.

243. Delong, Arthur R. "The Relative Effectiveness of Two Methods of Teaching Social Science at the College Level," University of Michigan, 1949. Unpublished doctoral dissertation, *Microfilm Abstracts,* 1949, 9, 162.
    Comparison of a "logical" vs. a "psychological" approach which stressed student's immediate interest and abilities.

244. Faw, Volney. "A Psychotherapeutic Method of Teaching Psychology," *American Psychologist,* 1949.
    Conducted at Lewis and Clark College.

245. Gross, Llewellyn. "Experimental Study of Validity of Non-Directive Method of Teaching," *Journal of Psychology,* 26, 1948.
    Conducted at University of Buffalo.

246. Johnson, Donald M. and Smith, Henry Clay. *Democratic Leadership in the College Classroom.* #361, Psychological Monographs. Washington: American Psychological Association, Inc., 1953.

247. Landsman, Theodore. "An Experimental Study of a Student-Centered Learning Method," Unpublished doctoral dissertation, Syracuse University, 1950.
    Conducted at Syracuse University.

248.   McKeachie, Wilbert J. "Individual Conformity to Attitudes of Classroom Groups," *Journal of Abnormal and Social Psychology*, 49, April 1954.
      Experimental study at University of Michigan.
249.   ———. "Student-Centered vs. Instructor-Centered Instruction," *Journal of Educational Psychology*, 1954.
      Reviews and carefully evaluates the present state of research on this subject.
250.   Rogers, Carl R. "Implications of Recent Advances in Prediction and Control of Behavior," *Teachers College Record*, February 1956.
251.   Wieder, Gerald S. "Group Procedures Modifying Attitudes of Prejudice in the College Classroom," *Journal of Educational Psychology*, 1954.
      Conducted at New York University
252.   Wispe, Lauren. "Evaluating Section Teaching Methods in the Introductory Course," *Journal of Educational Research*, November 1951.
      Outcomes of permissive vs. directive methods of teaching introductory course in Social Relations at Harvard University.

B. THE DISCUSSION METHOD

(122)   Bloom, Benjamin S. "Changing Conceptions of Examining at University of Chicago."
255.   ———. "Thought-Processes in Lectures and Discussion," *Journal of General Education*, 7, 1953.
      Experiment in stimulated recall at University of Chicago.
256.   ———. "The Thought-Processes of Students in Discussion," in French, Sidney J. (ed.) *Accent on Teaching*. New York: Harper & Brothers, 1954.
257.   Eglash, Albert. "Group-Discussion Method of Teaching Psychology," *Journal of Educational Psychology*, 1954.
      Study at Michigan State University.
258.   Guetzkow, Harold, Kelley, E. Lowell and McKeachie, W. J. "An Experimental Comparison of Recitation, Discussion and Tutorial Methods in College Teaching," *Journal of Educational Psychology*, 45, April 1954.
      Conducted in the introductory course in psychology at the University of Michigan.
259.   Hayes, Albert McHarg (ed.) "The Discussion Method in Teaching: A Symposium," *Journal of General Education*, 8, October

1954. Articles by Justus Buchler, Charles Wegener, Oliver S. Loud, Theodore M. Greene, and Joseph J. Schwab.

Buchler and Greene give effective arguments (though no empirical evidence) on the advantages of discussion as a means of liberal education.

C. The Problems Approach. Laboratory Practices in Social Science

261. Aldrich, Julian C. "Developing Critical Thinking," *Social Education*, March 1948.

Social science introductory sequence at New York University.

262. Burkhart, James A. and Tyrrell, William G. "Teaching Techniques, Non-Written Materials, and Classroom Procedures," in Tyrrell, William G. (ed.) *Social Studies in the College: Programs for the First Two Years*. Washington: National Council for the Social Studies, 1953.

263. Citizenship Education Project, Teachers College, Columbia University.

Evaluation data on the effects of introducing 'laboratory practices' in citizenship and other social science courses in schools and some colleges (30).

(53) Cook, Lloyd and Cook, Elaine. *Intergroup Education*.

(165) Cooke, Lawrence S. "An Analysis of Certain Factors Which Affect Student Attitudes Toward a Basic College Course, Effective Living."

264. Fersh, George L. (ed.) *The Problems Approach and the Social Studies*. Washington: National Council for the Social Studies, 1955. Curriculum Series Number Nine.

(124) Fersh, George L. "Changes in Social Beliefs and Social Values Effected by a Social Studies Course Based on the Problems Approach."

(129) Jones, O. Garfield. "Is Civic Education a Fraud?"

(279) Kennedy, Gail (ed.) *Education at Amherst: The New Program*.

Considers new curriculum a good first step toward education through active student participation in projects. Discusses problems approach in American Studies course. Predicts a "clinical" method of teaching.

265. Pringle, Henry F. and Pringle, Katharine. "School for Ultramodern Girls," *Saturday Evening Post*, 228, October 1, 1955. (Bennington College).

(35) Reed, Thomas H. and Reed, Doris D. *Evaluation of Citizenship Training and Incentive in American Colleges and Universities*.

(36) ———. *Preparing College Men and Women for Politics.*
266. Taylor, George R. *Report on Student Evaluation of American Civilization Course.* Mimeographed paper, Amherst College, 1956.

D. TEACHING BY TELEVISION

267. American Council on Education. *Teaching by Closed-Circuit Television.* Report of a Conference Sponsored Jointly by the Committee on Television of the American Council on Education and the State University of Iowa, Iowa Continuation Center, Iowa City, February 26–28, 1956. Washington: American Council on Education, 1956.
268. Carpenter, C. R. and Greenhill, L. P. and others. *An Investigation of Closed Circuit Television for Teaching University Courses. Instructional Television Research,* Project Number One. University Park, Pennsylvania: Pennsylvania State University, 1955. Sponsored by Fund for Advancement of Education; conducted by Instructional Film Research Program, with Pennsylvania State University.
269. Morris, John B. "Critical Thinking Gains and Achievement in a Social Science Course," unpublished memorandum, Syracuse University.

E. OTHER APPRAISALS OF TEACHING METHODS, especially as related to general education and the social sciences

270. American Political Science Association. *Goals for Political Science,* Report of the Committee for the Advancement of Teaching. New York: William Sloane Associates, Inc., 1951. Chap. X, Modernizing Teaching Methods.
(239) Tead, Ordway. *Character Building and Higher Education.*
272. Umstattd, James Greenleaf. *Teaching Procedures Used in Twenty-Eight Midwestern and Southwestern Colleges and Universities. Austin:* University Cooperative Society, 1954.
273. Wispe, Lauren. "Teaching Methods Research," *American Psychologist,* April 1953.

VI. VALUE PROFILES OF PARTICULAR INSTITUTIONS

279. Amberst College: Kennedy, Gail (ed.) *Education at Amherst: The New Program.* New York: Harper & Brothers, 1955.

280. Antioch College: Churchill, Ruth. "Evaluation of General Education at Antioch College," Chap. III in Dressel, Paul L. *Evaluation in General Education* (200).

281. ———: Studies by the Office of Testing and Evaluation, unpublished manuscripts.
    (1) Performance on various achievement tests of high and low scorers on the Inventory of Beliefs (1).
    (2) Personality traits and college adjustment of high vs. low scorers on Inventory of Beliefs.

282. ———: *Report to the Rockefeller Foundation on a Study of the General Education Program of Antioch College.* Otto F. Mathiasen, Director. Mimeographed paper, 1952–1953.

283. Beloit College: *Liberal Education at Beloit College.* A Report to the Faculty by the Committee on Self-Study. Beloit, Wisconsin, 1953.

(85) Bennington College: Newcomb, Theodore M. *Personality and Social Change: Attitude Formation in a Student Community.*

284. Brooklyn College: *Final Report of Ford Evaluation Study.* Brooklyn College, January 1, 1954.

285. University of Chicago: Bradbury, William. *Education and Other Aspects of Personal Growth in the College Community.*

(75) Colgate University: ACE Inventory of Beliefs and other tests administered to freshmen and readministered at end of sophmore year.

(9) Cornell University: Goldsen, Rose K. *Report on the Cornell Student Body.*

286. Harvard University: Funkenstein, Daniel, King, Stanley H. and Drolette, Margaret. *Mastery of Stress,* Harvard University Press, (In Press).
    An intensive experimental study of personality characteristics and values of undergraduates at selected private institutions.

(163) State University of Iowa: Carnegie Endowment for International Peace. *Universities and World Affairs.* Mimeographed paper. Document No. 80: The State University of Iowa and World Affairs.

(5) University of Louisville, Kentucky: Levi, Albert. *General Education in the Social Studies.* Chaps. 3 and 4.

(5) Macalester College: Levi, Albert. *General Education in the Social Studies.* Tables, Chap. 3; Chap. 6.

287. Michigan State University: Board of Examiners. Analyses of tests administered to freshmen at entrance; also to samples of upperclassmen, including various forms of the Inventory of Beliefs,

Critical Thinking in Social Science, Humanities Participation and other ACE and locally developed tests.

(74) ————: Carlin, Edward, Nosow, Sigmund and others. Study of outcomes of the introductory social science course in the Basic College (in process).

(5) ————: Levi, Albert. *General Education in the Social Studies.* Chap. 7; Tables, Chap. 3.

288. ————. Spacie, Edward. "Analysis of characteristics of middle-scorers on ACE Inventory of Beliefs," Michigan State University, doctoral dissertation in process, 1955–1956.

(87) Princeton University: Study of undergraduates throughout their college career.

(173, 223, 237) San Francisco State College. Office of Curriculum Evaluation. *Evaluation Reports.*

(88) Sarah Lawrence College. Studies of the development of student personality and attitudes during their college career.

(114) Southwestern at Memphis: *The Study of Values: Final Report.*

(71) Springfield College: Arsenian, Seth. "Changes in Evaluative Attitudes."

(191) Syracuse University: Downie, N. M., Troyer, M. E. and Pace, C. R. "The Knowledge of General Education of a Sample of Syracuse University Students as Revealed by the Cooperative General Culture Test and the Time Magazine Current Affairs Test."

(192) ————. "The Opinions of Syracuse University Students on Some Widely Discussed Current Issues."

(193) ————. "Problems in General Education Suggested by a Study of the Achievement and the Opinions of Syracuse University Students."

(194) ————. "A Study of General Education at Syracuse University with Special Attention to the Objectives."

(41) ————: Hall, Roy M. *Religious Beliefs and Social Values of College Students.*

(109) ————: Katz, Daniel and Allport, Floyd H. *Students' Attitudes.*

(289) ————: Pace, C. Robert. "Opinion and Action: A Study in Validity of Attitude Measurement," *Educational and Psychological Measurement,* 10, 1950.

(112) ————. "University-Wide Studies in Evaluation of General Education."

(34) ————. "What Kind of Citizens Do College Graduates Become?"

290. ————: *Self-Survey, Report,* 1949.

(306) Syracuse University: Stern, George G., *Studies in Personality Typologies.*

(146) —— and Cope, Alfred. Effects of personality on educational accomplishment.

(65) ——: Wallace, Donald G. "A Description and Interpretation of the Activities and Opinions of Syracuse Graduates Related to General Education."

(89) Vassar College: "Mellon Project."

(116) Wesleyan University: Special analysis of Wesleyan students' responses on the Cornell Values Survey.

291. Other. Funkenstein, D. H., Wechsler, H. and Merrifield, J. F., Unpublished data.

VII. PERSONALITY DETERMINANTS OF EDUCATIONAL OUTCOMES

(50) Allport, Gordon W. *The Nature of Prejudice.*

(51) —— and Kramer, Bernard M. "Some Roots of Prejudice."

300. Bills, Robert. "Effect of a Value on Learning," *Journal of Personality,* 1952.
Students who share the values of the instructor learn better (and perform better on examinations, even objective-type examinations).

(122) Bloom, Benjamin S. "Changing Conceptions of Examining at the University of Chicago."

(256) ——. "The Thought-Processes of Students in Discussion."

301. Corey, Stephen M. "Psychological Foundations of General Education," Chap. 3 in Henry, Nelson B. *The Fifty-First Yearbook of the National Society for the Study of Education.* op. cit. (166).

(12) Cross-Cultural Research Group. *Progress Report, No. 2,* December 1955.

302. Dexter, Emily S. "Personality Traits Related to Conservatism and Radicalism," *Character and Personality,* 7, 1939. (Agnes Scott College).

303. Evans, Richard I. "Personal Values as Factors in Anti-Semitism," *Journal of Abnormal and Social Psychology,* 47, 1952.

(167) Farnsworth, Dana, Funkenstein, Daniel H. and Wedge, Bryant. "The Social and Emotional Adjustment of 'Early Admission' College Students."

(107)   Fischer, Robert P. and Andrews, Avonne L. "Effect of Conformity to Social Expectancy on Evaluative Attitudes."

304.   Friedenberg, Edgar L. and Roth, Julius A. *Self-Perception in the University: A Study of Successful and Unsuccessful Graduate Students.* Supplementary Educational Monographs No. 80. Chicago: University of Chicago Press, January 1954.

(286)   Funkenstein, Daniel H., King, Stanley H. and Drolette, Margaret. *Mastery of Stress.*

(108)   Havighurst, Robert J. "Moral Character and Religious Education."

305.   Lecky, Prescott. *Self-Consistency, A Theory of Personality.* New York: Island Press, 1945.

(110)   Marcuse, F. L. "Attitudes and Their Relationships."

(133)   Morris, John B. "Critical Thinking Gains and Achievement in a Social Science Course."

(85)   Newcomb, Theodore M. *Personality and Social Change: Attitude Formation in a Student Community.*

(203)   Ostlund, Leonard A. "An Evaluation of a General Education Program."

(143)   Smith, Henry C. and Dunbar, Donald. "Personality and Achievement of Classroom Participant."

306.   Stern, George G. *Studies in Personality Typologies.* Mimeographed paper, based on speech to Midwest Psychological Association, 1953.

       Reports on experimental use of Inventory of Beliefs (Form T).

306a   ———. "Personality-Centered Research and Psychological Unification." *American Psychologist,* 8, 8, 1953.

(146)   ——— and Cope, Alfred. "Differences in Educability. . . ."

(15)   ———, Stein, Morris I and Bloom, Benjamin S. *Methods in Personality Assessment.*

(196)   Sternberg, Carl. *Personality Trait Patterns of College Students Majoring in Different Fields.*

307.   Stouffer, Samuel. "Analysis of Conflicting Social Norms," *American Sociological Review,* December 1949.

308.   Stouffer, Samuel and Toby, Jackson. "Role Conflict and Personality," *American Journal of Sociology,* 56, March 1951.

(146)   Syracuse University: Experimental study of effects of personality on educational accomplishment.

(16)   Todd, J. Edward. *Social Norms and the Behavior of College Students.*

309.   Goldberg, S., and Stern, G. G. "The Authoritarian Personality and General Education." *American Psychologist,* 7, 7, 1952.

VIII.   VALUE RESEARCH—METHODOLOGY AND
INSTRUMENTS

(50)   Allport, Gordon W. *The Nature of Prejudice.*

310.   ———, Vernon, Philip E. and Lindzey, Gardner. *Study of Values: Manual of Directions.* (revised ed.) New York: Houghton Mifflin Co., 1951.

311.   American Council on Education. Cooperative Study of Evaluation in General Education: *Attitudes Handbook.* Mimeographed paper.

312.   Bales, Robert F. *Value Profile.* Department of Social Relations, Harvard University.

313.   ———. "Factor Analysis of the Domain of Values in the Value Profile Test." Mimeographed paper, January 1956.

314.   Barron, Frank. *Inventory of Personal Philosophy.* University of California, Institute of Personality Assessment and Research. Berkeley: University of California Press, 1952.

315.   Diederich, Paul. *The "Critical Incidents" Technique Applied to Medical Education.* Research memorandum for the Educational Testing Service, Princeton, N. J., May 1954.

316.   ———. "Description of a Good Citizen." In Crary, Ryland W. (ed.) *Education for Democratic Citizenship,* Washington, D. C.: National Council for the Social Studies, 1951.

        Prepared for the U. S. Armed Forces Information and Education Division by a Committee of the National Council for the Social Studies and the U. S. Office of Education.

317.   Diederich, Paul. "Methods of Studying Ethical Development," *Religious Education,* I, 3 (May–June 1955) pp. 162–166.

318.   ———. "Studying the Development of Values," *Basic College Quarterly,* 1, Spring 1956.

319.   Divesta, Francis. "Process Concepts and Values in Social and Personal Adjustments of Adolescents." Memoir #287, Cornell University Agricultural Experiment Station, Ithaca, New York: November 1949.

(193) Downie, N. M., Pace, C. R. and Troyer, M. E. "Problems in General Education Suggested by a Study of the Achievement and Opinions of Syracuse University Students."

(200) Dressel, Paul L. *Evaluation in General Education.*

        Note especially chapters on evaluation at University of Chicago, San Francisco State College, and Syracuse University for analyses of methodological techniques.

320.   ———. "The Role of Evaluation in the Introductory College

Social Studies," in Tyrrell, William G. (ed.) *Social Studies in the College: Programs for the First Two Years.* op. cit. (262).

321. ——— and Mayhew, Lewis B. "Evaluation as an Aid to Instruction," Chap. 18 in French, Sidney J. *Accent on Teaching,* op. cit. (256).

(1) ———. *General Education: Explorations in Evaluation.*

322. Ehrmann, Henry W. "American Higher Education and the Social Sciences," Chap. 1 in *The Teaching of the Social Sciences in the United States.* Paris: UNESCO, 1954.

    Especially section on Ambiguities and Values in the Teaching of the Social Sciences, 29–33; Integration of the Social Sciences, 33–35.

(304) Friedenberg, Edgar L. and Roth, Julius A. *Self-Perception in the University: A Study of Successful and Unsuccessful Graduate Students.*

323. Jahoda, Marie and Havel, Joan. "Psychological Problems of Women in Different Social Roles," *Educational Record,* 36, October 1955.

(195) Knapp, Robert H. and Greenbaum, Joseph J. *The Younger American Scholar: His Collegiate Origins.*

324. McKeachie, Wilbert and Guetzkow, Harold. "A Rating-Ranking Scale for Goals of Life," *Religious Education,* 47, January–February 1952.

325. Murphy, Gardner, Murphy, Lois and Newcomb, Theodore. "Social Attitudes and Their Measurement," Chap. 13 in their *Experimental Social Psychology,* An interpretation of Research upon the Socialization of the Individual. New York: Harper & Brothers, 1937.

326. Naftalin, Arthur E., Hawley, Claude E. and Nelson, Benjamin. "The Social Sciences," in Morse, H. T. (ed.) *General Education in Transition: A Look Ahead.* op. cit. (235).

(204) Pace, C. Robert. "Evaluating the Outcomes of General Education."

(289) ———. "Opinion and Action: A Study in Validity of Attitude Measurement."

327. Pepitone, Albert and Reichling, George. "Group Cohesiveness and the Expression of Hostility," *Human Relations,* 8, 1955.

328. Reicken, Henry W. *The Volunteer Work Camp: A Psychological Evaluation.* Cambridge: Addison-Wesley Press, 1952.

329. ———. "Memorandum on Program Evaluation." Mimeographed paper.

(250)   Rogers, Carl R. "Implications of Recent Advances in Prediction and Control of Behavior."

330.   Schlesser, George E. *Personal Values Inventory*. Colgate University, 1952.

331.   Smith, Eugene R., Tyler, Ralph W. and Evaluative Staff. *Appraising and Recording Student Progress*. Vol. III of Adventure in American Education. New York: Harper & Brothers, 1942.

(15)   Stern, George G., Stein, Morris E. and Bloom, Benjamin S. *Methods in Personality Assessment*.

(308)   Stouffer, Samuel A. and Toby, Jackson. "Role Conflict and Personality."

(240)   Williams, Cornelia D., Eckert, Ruth E. and Potthoff, Edward F. "Basic Considerations in Planning Research in General Education."

IX.   SELECTED CRITIQUES OF GENERAL EDUCATION AND ITS OBJECTIVES

(1–5)   American Council on Education. *Cooperative Study of General Education*.

340.   American Society for Engineering Education. "Report of Committee on Engineering Education After the War," *Journal of Engineering Education*, 34, May 1944.

341.   ————. *Report on Evaluation of Engineering Education, 1952–1955*. Urbana, Illinois, 1955.

342.   Brown, Francis J. (Issue Editor) Issue on the Report of the President's Commission on Higher Education. *Journal of Educational Sociology*, April 1949:
   Russell, John Dale. "Basic Conclusions and Recommendations of the President's Commission on Higher Education."
   Farrell, Allan R. "Report of the President's Commission: A Critical Appraisal."
   Havens, Paul Swain. "Another Way Out?"
   McConnell, T. R. "A Reply to the Critics."
   Brown, Francis J. "Next Steps in Implementation."

343.   Christian Colleges, Report of the First Quadrennial Convention of, Denison University, Granville, Ohio, June 20–24, 1954, *The Christian Scholar*, Supplement, Autumn 1954.
   Note especially:
   Reeves, Marjorie. "Christian College in the Western World."

Lowry, Harold. "The Christian College as Christian Community."

Calhoun, Robert L. "Christian Vocation on the College Campus."

Seminar Report. "What the Christian Educational Community Requires in the Life of the Campus."

(199) Derbigny, Irving A. *General Education in the Negro College.*

(123) Eckert, Ruth E. *Outcomes of General Education.*

(201) Edgar, Earl E. "Values, Social Science and General Education."

344. Elbert, John A. "Weak Spots in the Harvard Report," *Catholic Educational Review,* 43, 1945.

345. Harvard University: *General Education in a Free Society.* Report of the Harvard Committee. Cambridge: Harvard University Press, 1945.

346. Henry, Nelson B. (ed.) *The Fifty-First Yearbook of the National Society for the Study of Education.* Part I: General Education. Chicago: University of Chicago Press, 1952.

347. Hochwalt, Frederick G. "Catholic Education in the U. S. A.," *Religious Education,* 48, September 1953.

348. Massachusetts Institute of Technology. *Report of the Committee on General Education,* 1949.

349. Moberly, Sir Walter. *The Crisis in the University.* London: SCM Press, 1949.

350. Morse, H. T. (ed.) *General Education in Transition: A Look Ahead.* Minneapolis: University of Minnesota Press, 1951.

351. Rattigan, Bernard Thomas. *A Critical Study of the General Education Movement.* Washington: Catholic University of America Press, 1952.

352. *Sibley, Elbridge.* "The Place of Social Science in General Education," *Journal of General Education,* October 1946.

353. Smith, Huston. *The Purposes of Higher Education.* New York: Harper & Brothers, 1955.

354. U. S. President's Commission on Higher Education. *Higher Education for American Democracy, A Report.* New York: Harper & Brothers, 1948.